DAVID WENTZ

Pastoring Revival

What to Do After the Holy Spirit Moves

DOING CHRISTIANITY
Pastor David Wentz

First published by Doing Christianity 2023

Copyright © 2023 by David Wentz

All rights reserved. No part of this publication may be reproduced, stored or transmitted in any form or by any means, electronic, mechanical, photocopying, recording, scanning, or otherwise without written permission from the publisher. It is illegal to copy this book, post it to a website, or distribute it by any other means without permission.

David Wentz asserts the moral right to be identified as the author of this work.

David Wentz has no responsibility for the persistence or accuracy of URLs for external or third-party Internet Websites referred to in this publication and does not guarantee that any content on such Websites is, or will remain, accurate or appropriate.

Scriptures marked NLT are taken from the HOLY BIBLE, NEW LIVING TRANSLATION (NLT): Scriptures taken from the HOLY BIBLE, NEW LIVING TRANSLATION, Copyright© 1996, 2004, 2007 by Tyndale House Foundation. Used by permission of Tyndale House Publishers, Inc., Carol Stream, Illinois 60188. All rights reserved. Used by permission.

Scriptures marked NAS are taken from the NEW AMERICAN STANDARD (NAS): Scripture taken from the NEW AMERICAN STANDARD BIBLE®, copyright© 1960, 1962, 1963, 1968, 1971, 1972, 1973, 1975, 1977, 1995 by The Lockman Foundation. Used by permission.

Scriptures marked NIV are taken from the NEW INTERNATIONAL VERSION (NIV): Scripture taken from THE HOLY BIBLE, NEW INTERNATIONAL VERSION ®. Copyright© 1973, 1978, 1984, 2011 by Biblica, Inc.TM. Used by permission of Zondervan

Scriptures marked ESV are taken from the THE HOLY BIBLE, ENGLISH STANDARD VERSION (ESV): Scriptures taken from THE HOLY BIBLE, ENGLISH STANDARD VERSION ® Copyright© 2001 by Crossway, a publishing ministry of Good News Publishers. Used by permission.

First edition

ISBN: 978-1-7331285-8-2

This book was professionally typeset on Reedsy.
Find out more at reedsy.com

*Dedicated to all who pray and work for revival,
and to pastors everywhere.*

Won't you revive us again, so your people can rejoice in you?

— Psalm 85:6 NLT

Contents

Foreword   iii
Preface   vii
Acknowledgement   ix
Introduction   x

I   Part 1: Revival! What It Is and What It Does

   1   What Exactly Are We Talking About? Terms and Definitions   3
   2   Revivals in History: Learning from the Experience of Others   14
   3   Unusual Behaviors: Validation, Distraction, or Deception?   25

II   Part 2: Three Case Studies

   4   Case Study 1: Rock City Church of Baltimore   45
   5   Case Study 2: The Crossing   71
   6   Case Study 3: The Author's Experience   88

III   Part 3. Pastoring Revival: Shepherding the Flock Without Getting in God's Way

   7   Pastoring a Move of God — Isn't That Presumptuous?   119
   8   Acquiring the Fire: Pastoring to Prepare for Revival   125
   9   Guarding the Flame: Pastoring During Revival   135

10	Don't Water the Spark: Avoiding Revival Killers	162
11	Putting It All Together	171

Appendix: Foundational Principles   179
About the Author   183
Also by David Wentz   185

Foreword

I am a professor of church renewal at a mainline Protestant seminary in Ohio. One of my jobs and specialties is renewal or revival in the life of the church. I study and teach on the history and theology of revival in Christianity. My students are mostly pastors, though not exclusively. In the class, we attempt to define and distinguish key words, like "revival," "renewal," "awakening," "outpouring," and "revitalization." We read about the Jesus movement of the first-century church, which was in one sense a Jewish renewal movement. We study early Christian renewal movements, in the first few centuries, like Montanism and various orders of Monasticism. We learn in revival how God reemphasizes for the church key themes like the Holy Spirit, discipleship, and life together. We learn about the various Reformation(s) in the fifteenth and sixteenth centuries, and how God is always reviving and reforming the church, shaping it according to his perfect will.

We also engage early modern revival movements. We learn about Pietism, Moravianism, Methodism, the First and Second Great Awakenings, and the Holiness and Healing revivals of the nineteenth century and God's restored emphasis on themes, such as repentance, the new birth, small groups, mission, scriptural holiness, and divine healing. We learn about the seismic moves of the Spirit of God in the twentieth century with the awakening in Wales, the Azusa St. revival, the Korean Pentecostal (Pyongyang Revival), the Mukti Revival in India, independent and indigenous outbreaking of the Spirit in Africa, the Methodist Pentecostal revival in Chile, the post-WWII healing revivals, the Latter-Rain movement of the gifts of the Spirit, the Charismatic renewal movement among Catholics and Protestants, the Jesus movement among the flower power generation of the late 1960s and early 1970s, and the ensuing so-called third wave of the Spirit among evangelicals.

All of these movements though different in many ways, put a needed primacy on the person and work of the Holy Spirit including the gifts of the Holy Spirit in the life of the church and in mission. The Lord restores the church's understanding of the person and power of the Spirit in our private lives, in ministry, worship, and mission, which often gets lost on us. The Spirit restores lives, his church, mission, and even society.

Finally, we examine the more recent outpouring of the Holy Spirit in the Global South and even in the West, including the revival fire that spread across many churches in the mid-1990s, including God's work in Toronto, Brownsville, Smithton (MO.), and other places. Even today, we are experiencing a fresh outpouring of the Spirit that began at Asbury University and has spread to other Christian and secular schools, churches, and other surprising places.

We spend considerable time in the classroom learning from these great moves of God. We learn what the church did right, and what it did wrong. We learn the various causes, effects, and impact of revival on the church and the world. We study the theological significance of these waves of the Spirit. We also learn to discern which phenomena in revival are essential and non-essential and also which are of God and not of God. We analyze revival from A to Z. Many Christian colleges, universities, and seminaries do not study the history and theology of revival. Revival may not be a part of their heritage or current practice, and/or they do not find it a subject worthy of their study. Thus, such an academic undertaking is rare and yet needed.

However, even though such research is warranted and invaluable, it is not enough. Revival by its very nature needs to be *tasted and experienced*. Otherwise, we truly do not *understand* what revival is. We can know every item on the menu of our favorite restaurant. We can know all of the prices of each item, and how each item is made. Perhaps, if skilled enough, we can even cook each item. We can be experts and connoisseurs of this restaurant's cuisine, and yet, unless we sit down and partake of each dish, then we really do not *know* the food. We do not know what it tastes like. We just analyze and speak from afar. We need to taste and see in order to know. It is the same with revival and the person and work of the Holy Spirit. We can study these topics thoroughly and exhaustively, but until we experience the life-changing power of the Holy Spirit in revival, then we do not *know* revival.

Many want revival. Many claim they know and understand revival enough to critique it. But very *few* have experienced it. As a professor, I have been blessed to not only understand revival academically but also to have experienced it spiritually in my own life, as a pastor and as a revivalist. The church I pastored in the 1990s and 2000s experienced the same wave of revival that hit Toronto, Brownsville, and other sites in America. The outpouring that showered upon our church in that time was beyond explanation. People were coming from all over the tri-state area to this little inner-city church that was landlocked in a small dying neighborhood and had no parking lot. People were transformed, healed, delivered, saved, sanctified, baptized in the Spirit, speaking in tongues, slain in the Spirit, ministering in the Spirit, witnessing angelic visitations, baptized in holy laughter, called into ministry, and you name it. I had never witnessed anything like it before or since.

Thus, it was often more of an art than a science to navigate through this tsunami of the Spirit's blessing. We saw it all, the good, the bad and the ugly. We saw the Spirit, the flesh, and the devil. Revival brings everyone's messy life together under the torrents of the Spirit's cleansing flood. It brings out things you want to see and things you do not want to see. Revival, beautiful as it is, can be messy, and at times even not so beautiful. Pastoring through such a once-in-a-lifetime journey can be challenging.

David Wentz has written a timely and accessible book for the season that the church is experiencing. Revival is breaking out in individual lives, churches, Christian schools and universities, secular universities, movie theaters, and other public spaces. What do you do when revival comes to you, your church, your school, or your town? In a lay version of his doctoral dissertation, the author shares wisdom from past and present on the nature of revival and how to pastor a reviving work of God. His aim is to help ministers lead effectively and safely through times of revival. Revival does not come often. We are not trained for it in seminary or in the pew, but when it does come, it takes you by surprise. God does an unprecedented new thing in a new way. And likewise, other unintended, unexpected surprises emerge. Often many of these unanticipated consequences arise from the human side of revival and even from the demonic side. A fire or a tornado does not happen frequently, but when it does it turns things upside down. So, we prepare thoroughly for this rare occasion, knowing that when it hits, there is little time to prepare. *Pastoring Revival* helps prepare us. This book offers clergy and lay leadership practical wisdom and guidance on how to steer the ship of the church effectively and safely through times of revival. On the wake of the Asbury Revival, I cannot think of a better time than now for the release of this book.

Rev. Peter J. Bellini Ph.D.
   Professor of Church Renewal and Evangelization in the Heisel Chair
   United Theological Seminary
   Dayton, Ohio

Preface

[Elisha] said, "Thus says the Lord, 'Make this valley full of trenches.' For thus says the Lord, 'You shall not see wind nor shall you see rain; yet that valley shall be filled with water, so that you shall drink, both you and your cattle and your beasts.'"
— 2 Kings 3:16–17 NAS

The kings of Judah, Israel, and Edom had been marching their armies through the desert for seven days with no water. They finally came to a stream bed. It was dry.

In desperation, they consulted the prophet Elisha, who gave them the above direction and promise from God. That night God must have sent rain in the nearby mountains, because the next morning they found that a flash flood had rolled through and filled the trenches with water.

If the leaders had not, by faith, put in the hard work of digging in the dry ground, the life-giving water would have passed right on by. Their faithful and persistent obedience is what allowed them to receive and benefit from the blessing God sent.

May this book be your blueprint for the spiritual irrigation trenches your church needs, so when God sends a flood of living water, you can receive and use it to his glory.

Happy digging!

Note: Your Bible may render this verse differently. The Hebrew verb is an infinitive absolute, which means God may be instructing the kings to dig or he may be promising to do the digging himself. The best translations are divided on this.

Both understandings can relate to revival. Sometimes God sends a flood of living waters unexpectedly, when the pastor and church haven't made any special preparations. More often, though, I believe God sends it where he knows the church has dug spiritual trenches, so they're ready to receive an outpouring of the Holy Spirit and conserve the fruit.

Acknowledgement

This book would not have been possible without the help, encouragement, and contributions of a number of people. In no particular order they include:

- Dr. Stephen A. Seamands, my advisor over two decades ago for the Doctor of Ministry dissertation which is at the core of this book
- Dr. Peter J. Bellini, who honored me by writing the Foreword
- Bishop Bart Pierce, senior pastor of Rock City Church of Baltimore, who allowed me to interview him, his staff, and his laypeople
- Evangelist Tommy Tenney, who graciously answered many questions
- Dr. Scott McDermott, senior pastor of Washington Crossing United Methodist Church ("The Crossing"), who granted me access to himself, his staff, and his laypeople, and invited me behind the scenes
- Staff members and laypeople at Rock City Church and The Crossing, who answered my questions and shared their testimonies
- Madison Pierce, who permitted me to include his insightful first-person observations of the 2023 Asbury outpouring
- Duane Steward, whose astute observations led to an almost complete rewrite, making this a much better book than it otherwise would have been
- Most of all, my wonderful wife, Paula, without whose love, support, and suggestions none of this would have come about

Introduction

Revival is a fire.

- It's a hearth that warms hearts and churches
- It's a stove that nourishes souls and spirits
- It's a furnace that consumes fluff and debris
- It's a smelter that refines and tempers character
- It's a boiler that powers growth and ministry

Revival can be a lightning bolt from God, a sudden strike of immense power, or it can be a carefully tended flame shared from one village to another. Revival can revitalize and energize a congregation and a community. That's why so many pastors seek it.

And revival can disrupt everything. Comfortable practices and long-held assumptions about how God does things can be turned upside down. That's why so many pastors are wary of it.

Revival almost always comes in response to earnest prayer. Many pastors pray for revival fervently and even publicly. When God answers those prayers, pastors celebrate. But sometimes those prayers are coming from laypeople, at home or in small groups, and the pastor doesn't know anything about them. When God answers *those* prayers, pastors can be blindsided.

Asbury

On February 8, 2023, something happened at Asbury University in the small town of Wilmore, Kentucky. As chapel ended and students began filing out, some stayed behind to pray. Others went to their classes but got permission to return to the chapel. Word got out that God was moving in a special way, and more students began to gather.

Two weeks later, round-the-clock prayer and worship had not stopped. Wilmore was jammed to the bursting point with people traveling from across America to experience it for themselves. Busloads of students from other Christian colleges attended for a few days, returned to their campuses, and saw similar outbreaks there.

Many saw it as the beginning of revival.

Revival is a sovereign move of God that only he can ignite. But as with most things God does, whether a revival will reach it's full potential largely depends on how God's people respond.

Consider: a body is the means by which the will of the head is made physical reality. We the church are the body of Christ, and Jesus is the head (Colossians 1:18). So the church is the means by which the will of Jesus is made physical reality.

And you, pastor, are in charge of how the local body of Christ in your care will do that. If God's will is to bring revival to your church, you are the one who has to pastor it.

What do I mean, "pastor it?"

Someone at Asbury had to decide whether to allow the students to stay in the chapel after the normal service was over. Then someone had to decide whether to allow them to remain there overnight. Someone had to decide whether to cancel classes. Someone had to decide who could use the microphones.

As word got out beyond the campus, someone had to decide how to handle visitors and what to do with inquiries from the media. Someone had to decide when and how to transition from round-the-clock worship services to something more normal. Above all, someone had to take responsibility for continual discernment of whether what was happening moment by moment was truly of God, and have a plan for what to do if something happened that was not.

At Asbury, "someone" was Dr. Kevin Brown, the president of the university. When it happens at your church, "someone" is you, the pastor. Making those decisions in a way that nurtures the move of God rather than quenching it is what I call pastoring revival.

Many believe revival is the only hope for our culture and our world. Many hope the events at Asbury were the beginning of it. As I write several months later, the institutional upheaval there is over, but what happened in people's hearts is just beginning to be seen.

Matt Brown wrote in *The Washington Times*, June 7, 2023,

> The spiritual clamor spread from Asbury to 37 other college campuses across the country that allowed young people to experience spiritual freedom, renewal and calling. There have been more than 200 teams of students testifying about the revival in churches since then, with hundreds more going out this summer. . . . And what happened at Asbury is only one example of the revival that is sweeping the nation.
>
> Pastor Robby Gallaty in Hendersonville, Tennessee, grew restless from the pressures of ministry in 2020 and he dedicated time on his porch to silent prayer for almost a year. Then he sensed God leading him to call for a spontaneous baptism at his church. That was a highly unusual concept with the way he normally did ministry, but he sensed it was God. So he did it.
>
> Over the next year, revival swept the church with more than 1,500 people expressing their faith through public baptism.
>
> And on May 28, 2023, on what is known as "Pentecost Sunday,"

> Pastor Mark Francey felt led to hold a public baptism at Pirates Cove, California, one of the sites of the Jesus Movement. He invited other churches to participate, and 280 churches from across Southern California came together.
>
> In total, 4,166 people were baptized at one time. This was the largest baptism in California history, and some people are calling it the largest baptism in American history.
>
> We are living through that moment right now. And there's more to come.

One example came in mid-September, 2023, at Auburn University in Alabama, as more than two hundred students were baptized in a campus lake in an impromptu service following a worship concert.

And it continues to happen.

It's not unusual for revivals to begin with scattered outbreaks. History implies a pattern of revivals coming in waves. It behooves us to be ready, because the next one seems to be rolling in.

What Do You Do When God Shows Up?

One definition of revival is when human initiative is replaced by divine initiative. In other words, as some put it, "God shows up." When people experience a sudden strong sense of God's presence in a church service, they can respond in a wide variety of ways. In fact, almost the only thing you can count on as pastor is that the service will be different than you had planned.

Maybe you're leading the congregation in prayer and suddenly everyone starts weeping. Or maybe some of your people just came back from visiting a revival, and in the middle of your sermon, they stand up and start loudly praising God. Perhaps you're quietly praying with someone and they suddenly slump to the floor under the power of the Holy Spirit. Or maybe you give your normal weekly altar call and half the church rushes forward, and after you've finished praying for them all, nobody wants to go home.

As pastor, what are you going to do?

Just as you should have a contingency plan for a fire or a medical emergency, you should have a contingency plan for revival. That's the purpose of this book.

Our subject is not how to bring revival to your church. This book is about what to do when it comes. As one pastor put it, "When God is moving, I want to know how to stay out of his way."

A big part of a pastor's job is to shepherd your flock through whatever God is doing, whether it's a financial crisis, a building program, the death of a beloved leader, or any of a thousand other things that happen to churches. This book is about how to shepherd them when the thing God is doing is revival.

I hope it will not only prepare you if God sends revival to your church, but make you pray that he will.

Been There, Done That, and Have the T-Shirt

Most of the major events of my Christian life and ministry have happened in the context of revival or its aftermath.

- I committed myself as a Christian in 1972 as part of the Jesus Revolution.
- Seven years later I attended seminary in Southern California where that "revolution" started.
- In the '90s I experienced and studied the River Movement that included the Toronto Awakening and the Brownsville Revival.
- I pastored a church experiencing many revival dynamics.
- I wrote my Doctor of Ministry dissertation on the subject of

pastoring revival.

I served as a pastor for 38 years, and I've helped train thousands of pastors through my books and lectures. I've been there, done that, and I literally have the T-shirts. I'm still hungry for more of God, and I'm still praying for revival.

Let me say right here that by using the terms "revival" or "the Spirit moves," I am not implying a better kind of ministry than the normal operation of a healthy church. I believe the local church, doing what God calls it to do, is the hope of the world, and I train pastors internationally to do that. In this book, I'm focusing on unusual revival experiences because history shows they happen periodically and recent events imply another is on the horizon, and there is very little written about how pastors should lead their churches through and after them.

The last big wave of revival in North America started in 1994, though there were precursors, as I believe what happened at Asbury and other colleges may be precursors of the next wave. Those involved in the '90s often referred to themselves as being "in the River," from Ezekiel 47 and Revelation 22. I had the privilege of being involved in that from three perspectives:

- As a visiting worshiper hoping to bring revival home
- As a pastor leading small but fervent groups of revived worshipers within several largely indifferent denominational congregations
- As a student doing case study research for my Doctor of Ministry dissertation, with the goal of learning how pastors of congregations in revival can sustain it while supporting other ongoing ministries. (You can find the original dissertation online at https://place.asburyseminary.edu/ecommonsatsdissertations/506/.)

This book draws from all three of those perspectives.

They Didn't Teach Me This in Seminary!

When pastors get together, one of their favorite games is, "They didn't teach me this in seminary!" Pastoring revival would be at the top of most lists.

The truth is, few pastors confronted with revival in their churches have ever experienced anything like it before. Even in denominations built on revival, most pastors have studied it as an event of the past and prayed for it as a hope for the future without ever having personally experienced it.

Some pastors shun anything that seems like "emotionalism" or "supernaturalism." They've been taught that these things don't happen anymore, if they ever did. If you are one who has been taught these things, thank you for being open-minded enough to read a book like this. After all, to talk about God is by definition to talk about the supernatural. And it's easy to confuse spiritual and emotional experiences because our language doesn't have good words to distinguish between the two.

There are four very natural human reactions to the unusual: deny it, avoid it, attack it, or try to control it. A decidedly un-natural reaction is a desire to pastor it. But when God brings revival to your church, that is exactly what you are called to do.

For many, all they know of "revival" is sensationalized reports of people jerking and shouting, barking like dogs, and falling to the floor. It's true that unusual behaviors have accompanied most historical revivals, and we'll look at that in a later chapter. It may reassure you to know that they have not been a focus of the Asbury outpouring, at least in its initial stages.

What Does It Look Like This Time Around?

What might you expect if what started at Asbury spreads to your church? I share with permission some observations by an informed participant. On day ten of the outpouring, Madison Pierce, a student of Asbury Seminary, wrote:

> *I'm hesitant to post my thoughts on what's happening in Wilmore. A few of you may have heard about the "Revival" at Asbury University. I attended the gatherings from the first day til now. A chapel service that didn't stop but continued spontaneously for 9 days now. It was an intimate space for students but it is now the focus of global intrigue, mass pilgrimage, and digital evaluation. I am aware that not everyone has a paradigm for this form of spirituality but I want to be honest to my own understanding.*
>
> *I come from a spiritual background that has left me weary of hype in a culture of spectacle. I've grown tired of disintegrous representations of divine work but it is clear God is moving in a surprising and transformative way. However, when you think of "revival", what comes to mind might not be what's happening.*
>
> *To quote Professor McCall, a theology professor at Asbury Seminary, "what we are experiencing now—this inexpressibly deep sense of peace, wholeness, holiness, belonging, and love—is only the smallest of windows into the life for which we are made."*
>
> *The movements of the Spirit in western evangelicalism always exist in the middle of a cultural moment. A generous interpretation of these movements reveals unique traits for each one. For example, fervor for the great commission at the Mt. Hermon Conference, overwhelming joy in Toronto Outpouring, zeal for the lost in Brownsville Revival, acts of healing at the Kansas City awakening, and manifestation of tongues at the Azusa Street revival. In each*

move of the Spirit, God clearly manifests in a specific way for that generation. I find it interesting that God would mark this [Asbury] outpouring with:

- *A tangible sense of peace for a generation with unprecedented anxiety*
- *A restorative sense of belonging for a generation amidst an epidemic of loneliness*
- *An authentic hope for a generation marked by depression*
- *A leadership emphasizing protective humility in relationship with power for a generation deeply hurt by the abuse of religious power*
- *A focus on participatory adoration for an age of digital distraction*

It feels as if God is personally meeting young adults in ways meaningful to them. My generation was formed differently than previous generations and so the traits of this revival are different than revivals of old. The new outpouring is not the signs and wonders nor zealous intercession nor spontaneous tongues nor charismatic physicalities nor the visceral travail. It is marked by a tangible feeling of holistic peace, a restorative sense of belonging, a non-anxious presence through felt safety, repentance driven by experienced kindness, humble stewardship of power, and holiness through treasuring adoration.

It is important to reflect on the words of Jesus "no one pours new wine into old wineskins. Otherwise, the new wine will burst the skins; the wine will run out and the wineskins will be ruined. No, new wine must be poured into new wineskins." [Mark 2:22]

I don't want to make the mistake of trying to fit this new work into old paradigms. The new wine cannot be understood with the old expectations of revival.

As the revival has grown, people attempt to evaluate and participate from their old expectations. You cannot keep new

> *wine in the old wineskin; or it may cause disappointment, disillusionment and divisiveness. In humility, we must receive the new wine with an open hand without trying to force this spiritual movement into our well-intended but old expectations of renewal. We must strive to humbly participate, appreciatively celebrate, and intentionally respond to this surprising work of the Spirit with openness and hunger.*

I so appreciate Madison's sensitive and astute observations. In this book, I don't want to be guilty of trying to force a new move of God into old wineskins. However, there are some timeless principles, because basic truths about God and human nature don't change. Our focus here is not on what revival should look like, but on how to nurture it, whatever form it takes.

Four Stages of Revival

Revival has four basic stages: an initial outpouring, tending the fire, spreading the spark, and preserving the fruit. This book is about the first two stages. It's designed for pastors who suddenly find their church hosting the Holy Spirit in a new and perhaps unsettling way, and those who want to.

Revival could strike your church out of the blue, hitting everyone in a worship service. That's what happened in the two churches I studied for my doctoral dissertation. You could seek personal revival for yourself and then try to introduce it to your church. That's what happened to me as a pastor. Or some of your people could catch revival fire, often through visiting a place where it has already broken out, and bring it back to your congregation. That may be the most common way revival has spread in the past. And often the pastors were caught off guard.

You may have picked up this book because such a thing has already happened in your church. Or perhaps someone gave it to you because they hope it will. If some of your people are claiming revival and you are not really sure about it, allow me to share a bit of advice given to pastors during the Jesus Revolution: a revival experience, in itself, does not make people better Christians than anyone else, but it may make them better Christians than they were before.

And if you let it, it may make you a better pastor than you were before.

After the fact, scholars and critics often look back and debate whether or not a given occurrence rose to the level of a "true revival." Most of that, of course, is a matter of definition, and everyone seems to have their own. As valuable as those discussions may be in academic circles, we won't be going there. This book is not for historians looking back. I was a pastor for thirty-eight years, and an engineer before that. My mindset is toward the practical and usable, and my heart is for the work of God.

As you have opportunity, I encourage you to read more on the subject of revival. A good place to start might be with those who pastored churches in the last wave such as John Arnott of the Toronto revival and John Kilpatrick of the Brownsville/Pensacola revival, and those from the "Jesus Revolution" of the 1960s and '70s such as Chuck Smith and John Wimber.

But when revival hits, you don't have time to wade through a lot of theological and historical analysis, as valuable as that may be. Therefore, the goal of this book is to provide you with quick access to experience-based advice. It's for pastors in the middle of things, trying to shepherd their flocks in real-time. I pray it helps you.

I

Part 1: Revival! What It Is and What It Does

Revive us so we can call on your name once more.
— Psalm 80:18 NLT

1

What Exactly Are We Talking About? Terms and Definitions

No standard set of words is consistently used to discuss the work and movement of God in churches and communities. Our focus in this book is those moves of God among Christians where some or all the people in a service sense an unusual and powerful presence of God that continues beyond the one service. Often this is accompanied by unusual emotional, mental, and even physical reactions. The most common terms used to refer to such happenings are "revival" and "outpouring," often used interchangeably.

Ephesians 5:18 commands us to be filled with the Holy Spirit. Jonathan Edwards viewed revival as an outpouring of the Holy Spirit. So revival is God's way of helping us obey that commandment.

Revival moves us from where we may have allowed ourselves to be, relying on our own human efforts, to where we ought to be. Given our human tendency to keep trying to do things by ourselves, most of us have a recurring need for revival.

In his book *The Day of Thy Power*, Arthur Wallis wrote,

> There is a wealth of difference between missions or campaigns

at their best and genuine revival. In the former man takes the initiative, it may be with the prompting of the Spirit; in the latter the initiative is God's. With the one the organization is human; with the other it is divine. . . . Revival is divine intervention in the normal course of spiritual things. It is God revealing Himself to man in awful holiness and irresistible power. It is such a manifest working of God that human personalities are overshadowed, and human programmes abandoned. It is man retiring into the background because God has taken the field. It is the Lord making bare His holy arm, and working in extraordinary power on saint and sinner. . . Revival must of necessity make an impact upon the community, and this is one means by which we may distinguish it from the more usual operations of the Holy Spirit.

What We're Not Talking About

Before we try to define things more exactly, perhaps I can calm some trepidations by stating what I am not talking about when I use the term "revival."

First, I'm not talking about pre-planned special services intended to motivate members and attract new converts. Tent revivals, camp meetings, and special services with guest speakers are all time-honored ways to do those things and I encourage you to use them as God leads, but these planned events are not our subject here.

Second, I'm not talking about emotionalism. When the Holy Spirit comes on a person, an emotional response of tears or joy or both is often one immediate result. But those emotions are human responses largely related to personality. Their presence or absence does not prove or disprove the presence and working of God.

Third, I'm not talking about unusual behaviors. People falling to the ground and other strange responses have been reported so often in revival history that I have devoted a full chapter to what they are and how to deal with them. As with emotion, however, these are largely human responses. They neither prove nor disprove revival.

So What Are We Talking About?

Amy Elizabeth Ward, a teenager at Brownsville Assembly of God in Pensacola, Florida, became widely known within the River movement of the 1990s through her testimony of a life-changing experience with Christ. Her youth pastor, Richard Crisco, asked her what revival meant to her. He recorded her answer in *It's Time: Passing Revival to the Next Generation*.

> She said that it means being able to go into God's presence. It means going into her room, shutting off all the lights, sitting quietly in the darkness, and feeling God there with her. Revival means to know God and to listen to God from her heart.

This is a far cry from the popular perception of revival. This is the inner transformation the church and the world need. Without such inner transformation, no revival is worthy of the name.

As of this writing, the main effect of what has been happening at Asbury and other colleges seems to be very similar to Amy Ward's testimony. The defining characteristic has been praise and worship, rather than sermons or evangelistic messages. One reason may be that it broke out in a Christian college with a heritage of revival. Most of the students, and most of those who traveled to be a part, recognized what was happening and welcomed it. As it has spread to secular campuses, an additional characteristic has been large numbers of students seeking baptism.

When visitors to revival sites seek to bring it back to their churches and enthusiastic revived students return home for the summer, not everyone will understand what they are talking about. Pastors must be ready to encourage the new and revived Christians, as well as help less fervent members of their congregations understand what is happening and encourage them to respond.

You may have had moving worship services where people felt a special presence of God. You may have had times when many came to the altar for prayer. You may have had a special series of meetings or services that breathed new life into your congregation. You may even have pastored services where "God showed up," and spiritual gifts and healings and miracles occurred. If your congregation has never experienced these things before, their sudden appearance could well be the start of revival. For many churches, however, this is more or less worship as usual. It's God and it's wonderful but it's not revival.

Revival, by definition, is unusual. It's disruptive. It can seem out of control, maybe even fanatical. That's why I say few pastors have experienced it before. Genuine, God-initiated, Christ-honoring, Holy Spirit-directed revival doesn't happen very often. When it does, it's transformative.

That's probably why there are so many poor imitations. My experience is similar to that of David Watson of United Theological Seminary, who posted this:

> *I have spent considerable time in revivalistic gatherings. Sometimes the Spirit's presence is undeniably manifest. Sometimes things feel contrived or manufactured. Sometimes God so fills the gathered faithful that they respond with tears, laughter, or cries of praise and thanksgiving. Sometimes affected emotionalism becomes a distraction. I've seen the good, the bad, and the ugly. The bad and the ugly are disappointing, at times painful, but the*

good is the life-changing presence of the one who is goodness itself.

Terms and Labels

Revival, renewal, awakening, outpouring, movement, and even "Jesus Revolution" are all terms that have been used to label our subject, along with phrases like "an anointed service," "a touch of God," or "God showed up."

Unfortunately, there is no agreed-upon set of definitions for these things. Pneumatology, the study of the Holy Spirit, is not settled theological ground like Christology, the study of Christ. Neither is it a well-rehearsed debate field like eschatology, the study of the end times. Both of those have settled terms and definitions. Revival, and pneumatology in general, doesn't.

Part of the reason may be that theologians just haven't gotten there yet. But I think a bigger factor is that words are symbols pointing to shared experiences, and in terms of how languages develop, not enough people have shared these experiences to have created a common vocabulary.

For the purposes of this book, then, here are the definitions I have in mind.

Church: a group of people who hold regularly scheduled religious services, usually led by a pastor and happening in a church building (though neither the pastor nor the building are necessary to the definition). I include chapels, retreat centers, and similar faith communities here. The level and quality of spiritual life and activity will vary widely, but this is the starting point, what you might call the pre-revival baseline.

Anointing: when the Holy Spirit operates through a sermon, song, or testimony to give it an unusually powerful effect on people. They may describe it as feeling a touch from God.

Manifest presence of God: when people have a spiritual sense of experiencing God's presence with them that goes beyond their intellectual belief in God's omnipresence.

Outpouring: when the Holy Spirit acts in such a way that there are widespread spiritual, emotional, and even physical responses beyond the norm for that church, and there is general agreement that God did something special. This is the word I would use to describe what happened at Asbury.

Revival: when an outpouring continues for an extended time and has a lasting effect on a church or region. This is probably the most common informal definition of revival. In the context of religion, the word has left behind its medical meaning of bringing new life into a comatose individual. Religious revival does bring new life, but it does not necessarily imply that the church was comatose before. Revival in this sense can come to and through churches whose spiritual vital signs are already excellent.

Movement: when God sends revivals with similar characteristics to a number of places in a relatively short time, such that their effects overlap and reinforce each other. If a movement is effectively organized so as to conserve its spiritual fruit, it can become a lasting feature of the religious landscape.

Awakening: a revival movement that overflows the church into the general population. Large numbers of people are awakened to spiritual realities, and the general society is positively affected.

Here are three examples.

1. The day of Pentecost began as an outpouring in the upper room that spread, with less dramatic manifestations, to the crowd in the streets of Jerusalem. It continued as a revival involving more and more citizens of Jerusalem. It became a movement spreading to other cities, and resulted in the awakening of Christian faith in

much of the population.
2. In the 1700s, the open-air preaching of John Wesley was often accompanied by an outpouring of the Holy Spirit, complete with emotional and physical responses. Over time the results of this came to be known as the Methodist Revival, which gave birth to the Holiness Movement. Historians group this with similar events accompanying the preaching of Jonathan Edwards and George Whitefield in what they call The First Great Awakening. Both Methodism and the Holiness Movement continue to be major forces in Protestant Christianity.
3. In 1906 an outpouring in a church service in Los Angeles became the Azusa Street Revival. As the revival spread it spawned the Pentecostal Movement, which has resulted in a worldwide awakening of faith, particularly in Africa and South America.

Before we move on, I'd like to mention three other "R" words sometimes used in this context.

- *Reformation* is a theological or ecclesiological correction, having to do with what we believe and how we do church. While certainly inspired by God through the Holy Spirit, reformation is primarily a divinely guided activity of the mind rather than a sovereignly granted experience of the spirit, though one can certainly lead to and reinforce the other.
- *Renewal* is a reversal of decay, a restoration of youthful energy and purity. Revival should result in spiritual renewal among those involved, demonstrated by increased holiness of lifestyle. If, after a reasonable period of time, it has not, there is cause to question whether the so-called revival was a true move of God. *You will know them by their fruits* (Matthew 7:16 NAS).
- *Revolution* is rebellion against an old system to replace it with a

new one, usually with the connotation of violence. While religion has been used as an excuse for violent change in the past, Jesus preferred to use metaphors such as yeast working quietly in a batch of dough, or a seed gradually growing into a large plant (see Matthew 13:31-33). The term "Jesus Revolution" was not coined by theologians or church historians seeking to describe a work of God, but by journalists hoping to sell magazines.

I praise God for every one of these ways he works (with the nuanced exception of violent revolutions). All are deserving of study. Of them all, however, an outpouring of God's Spirit and its possible extension into revival are the two that can have the biggest impact on a local church. Unfortunately, they are the ones most pastors are least prepared for. In earning two Master of Divinity degrees and a Doctor of Ministry from charismatic, mainline, and Wesleyan-evangelical seminaries, I never came across a course on how to pastor a church during an outpouring or revival. In fact, I don't recall even hearing it mentioned.

So that will be the focus of the rest of this book.

Working Definitions

It's time to be more specific. Here are expanded definitions of our two main topics.

Outpouring

> *An outpouring is a sovereign act of God in which, during an identifiable period of time, an identifiable group of people gives evidence of experiencing an unusual sense of God's presence and attributes such as God's love, power, conviction, mercy, joy, or*

forgiveness; often accompanied by supernatural manifestations such as healing and other 1 Corinthians 12 gifts of the Holy Spirit; and sometimes accompanied by physical reactions such as falling to the ground or unusual movements or vocalizations.

A sovereign act of God: We can pray for revival, and we can prepare for it, but we cannot cause it to happen. That is always up to God.

An identifiable period of time: Individual experiences of God are wonderful, and most pastors know how to guide parishioners who may report them. But when many people have such experiences at one time or in one church service, something different is going on, and few pastors are prepared for it.

An identifiable group of people: Again, not scattered reports of individual blessings, but something affecting many people at once; in particular, the congregation you, as pastor, are responsible for.

Unusual: Something beyond what you would normally expect for that group or setting.

Sense of God's presence and attributes: Not just intellectual understanding or mental assent to a doctrine, but a noticeable spiritual experience or sensation.

God's love, power, conviction, mercy, joy, or forgiveness: People may testify to God revealing himself to them in these ways and others.

Supernatural manifestations: People may report visions, revelations, healings, and other miracles.

Unusual movements or vocalizations: People may cry out, jerk, fall, or show other bodily responses. Chapter 3 will deal with these in detail.

Revival

> *Revival is when the effects of one or more outpourings expand beyond the initial setting to other churches, resulting in heightened spiritual awareness and activity for an extended period of time.*

Effects: The immediate effects of an outpouring are the responses of the people. Often these responses are emotional. That's not a bad thing; emotions are part of the soul. The Bible attributes a variety of emotions to Jesus, God the Father, and even the Holy Spirit. These responses often result in enthusiastic sharing with family and friends in other churches.

One or more outpourings: Revival can start with one outpouring, a series of outpourings in one church, or a series of outpourings in various places.

Expanding to other churches: God may choose to give an outpouring, or even a series of outpourings, to one congregation. When this happens, I believe it should best be taken as an early sign of a wave of revival to come, rather than revival itself. Outpouring becomes revival when it spreads.

Heightened spiritual awareness and activity: If what is experienced during an outpouring is truly from God and is truly received, it will make a difference. Part of pastoring revival is teaching and encouraging people to let the experience motivate them to become more devoted to prayer, worship, Bible reading, Christian fellowship, service, discipleship, and holiness of life.

Extended period of time: This is a purposely vague term, because every revival is different. What I mean is that if you visit the scene of a revival several years later, you should still be able to tell something happened there.

Now that we've narrowed down our subject matter, let's see how it has looked in the past, from the Bible through today.

2

Revivals in History: Learning from the Experience of Others

God almost never does the same thing the same way twice. God loves to do a new thing (Isaiah 43:19), and it is often said that the biggest obstacle to the next wave of God comes from people trying to make it look like the last one.

This can certainly be true. However, one of the most often repeated commands in the Bible is, "remember." *Now these things happened to them as an example, and they were written for our instruction, upon whom the ends of the ages have come* (1 Corinthians 10:11 NAS). The lessons of past revivals should instruct us as we prepare for the next one.

As we read the signs of the times and prepare ourselves for what God may be doing, it's important to learn what we can from what God has done before.

Revivals in the Bible

Revival is not a new phenomenon. It goes back to the early days of Bible history.

- Moses' demonstrations of God's power revived the spirits of the Israelites
- Judges narrates a repeating cycle of complacency, apostasy, trouble, revival, and complacency again
- King David led a revival in worship and faith, climaxing when he brought the ark to Jerusalem
- The good kings of Judah are identified as those who revived worship of the true God
- The religious fervor that caused Hebrew men to follow Ezra's call to put away foreign wives could certainly be called revival
- The great multitudes who thronged to hear John the Baptist and Jesus indicate revival
- The day of Pentecost, with three thousand souls added to God's kingdom in one day, is what many pastors imagine as they pray for revival
- Mass conversions under the preaching of Peter in Jerusalem after the healing of the lame man (Acts 3) and under Philip in Samaria (Acts 8) were obviously revivals
- At least three of Jesus' messages to the seven churches in Revelation are calls to revival: the warnings to Ephesus to return to their first love (Revelation 2:5), to Sardis to strengthen their faith (Revelation 3:2-3), and to Laodicea to recognize their true condition and take steps (Revelation 3:17-18)

In addition, the Bible records prayers such as, *Revive us so we can call on your name once more* (Psalm 80:18 NLT), and *Won't you revive us again, so your people can rejoice in you?* (Psalm 85:6 NLT).

Hosea 10:12 NLT reads, *Plow up the hard ground of your hearts, for now is the time to seek the Lord, that he may come and shower righteousness upon you.*

This verse describes a common pattern of revivals in Bible times and through history:

- *Plow up the hard ground of your hearts:* people become unsatisfied with the spiritual status quo
- *For now is the time to seek the Lord:* people seek revival through fervent prayer
- *That he may come and shower righteousness upon you:* God answers with a powerful outpouring of his Spirit

Revivals in Church History

From Bible times to the Reformation, many of those named saints of the church, such as St. Francis and St. Ignatius, were given that title because of their fervor for leading people beyond ritual to follow God in deeper ways. The monastic movements that bear their names are lasting testimony to the effects of their fervor. And while there were certainly doctrinal, ecclesiastical, and even political elements to the Reformation, probably the main factor in its lasting success was the revival of spirituality sparked by leaders such as Luther, Calvin, and Knox.

In the mid-1700s, revivals under Jonathan Edwards, the Wesleys, and George Whitefield sparked the First Great Awakening. A hundred years later, Charles Finney and the camp meeting preachers led the revivals of the Second Great Awakening. And we've already mentioned Azusa Street and the beginning of the Pentecostal movement in 1906.

Americans may not be as familiar with what God has done in other parts of the world. In the last century or so, revivals in Wales, East Africa, the Scottish Hebrides, and other places had major impacts that carry on to this day. And the growth of the church in South America and Africa has been nothing short of explosive.

The biggest revival in the lifetimes of most of those reading this was what the media named The Jesus Revolution. For about ten years starting in the late 1960s, millions of people, including me, experienced faith either for the first time or at a significantly deeper level. The commercial success of retrospectives such as The Jesus Revolution movie testify to the enduring effects of this move of God.

Now, with the Asbury outpouring, it appears that God may be doing it again.

But there was a significant move of God between the Jesus Movement and Asbury. Those involved called it The River. As the most recent major revival, at least in North America, it may be the one we can learn the most from.

The River Movement

In the mid-1990s, something began to happen in churches in the United States and around the world. Scandals, ethnic tension, and wars had caused many Americans to lose their faith in business, government, and the innate goodness and progress of humanity. Environmental problems, natural disasters, and a lack of progress against AIDS and other illnesses had destroyed confidence in technology and in intellectually-based solutions in general. A hunger arose for something different. The parallels with today are obvious.

Across the nation and around the world, God began to answer that hunger. The experiential reality of the presence of God, which is the unifying characteristic of every major revival in history, was manifested as seldom seen before. In the common phrase of what became a movement, the River of God was sweeping across our land.

Perhaps the most famous examples, at least in North America, were long-lasting revival meetings at the Toronto Airport Christian Fellowship in Ontario, Canada, and at Brownsville Assembly of God in Pensacola, Florida. Both of these churches held well-attended services at least five nights a week for several years, and received major mainstream media exposure. At the same time, more and more churches experienced similar occurrences, both in and outside the United States.

These outbreaks quickly merged into a movement. It had no formal structure, but those involved began to identify what was happening by saying they were "in the River." Dutch Sheets' excellent book, *The River of God*, explained and encouraged the movement using that imagery. Though the name never seemed to catch on outside the revival, within it the phrase became so well known that several worship songs were written about it, including "Let the River Flow," "The River Is Here," and "Find Me in the River."

For the next few pages we'll dive more deeply into the River than the cursory overviews we've given previous revivals. There are two reasons for this.

- The historical, cultural, and religious setting of the River is not far removed from what we experience today, so people's responses, both secular and Christian, may be similar.
- Some veterans of the River who are attracted to present-day outpourings may engage in the same physical responses as they did in the 1990s, because they believe that's what you do when revival comes. This was already experienced at Asbury. These learned responses — more about that in the next chapter — can get in the way of the new thing God wants to do, so pastors should be aware of them.

Much of Part 3 of this book is based on learnings from two pastors who successfully pastored their churches through the River, not only during the initial outpourings and active revival period, but in the decades since.

Outbreak of the River

The first widely recognized outbreak of the River in North America was the January 1994 visit of Baptist pastor Randy Clark to preach a series of services at the Toronto Airport Vineyard Christian Fellowship.

In what secular media dubbed "The Toronto Blessing," the Holy Spirit fell. Suddenly a large portion of the congregation found themselves filled with an overwhelming sense of joy, and broke out in what was dubbed "holy laughter." Many also fell to the floor in an experience already known in charismatic/Pentecostal circles as being "slain in the Spirit."

As these and other manifestations continued night after night, people began to come from not only the Toronto area but from around Canada and as far away as Hong Kong.

A year and a half later, on Father's Day, 1995, something similar happened at Brownsville Assembly of God in Pensacola, Florida. Outbreaks that received less attention in the secular media occurred at other churches, including Smithton Community Church in 1996, where a Pentecostal congregation of 180 members in a Missouri town with a population of 532 hosted over 250,000 visitors over the next three years; Rock City Church in Baltimore in 1997; and Washington Crossing United Methodist Church in Pennsylvania in 1998.

It was unusual for a revival service to be shorter than three hours, and five was not uncommon. Richard Crisco, youth pastor at Brownsville, wrote in his book *It's Time: Passing Revival to the Next Generation*,

> *People ask how we can do this night after night. How can we not do it night after night? Fish were made to swim in water. We were made to live like this. God wants us to live and move and have our being in Him, in His presence.*

Worship is the all-consuming activity of heaven. This was just a foretaste. Who would not like to spend several hours a night in heaven?

Most revivals have been identified with one or two major leaders, such as Jonathan Edwards, Charles Finney, or Wesley and Whitefield. By contrast, no one particular leader was in charge of the River. Rather than being the effect of an orchestrated promotion, the River had its source in numerous local pastors and prayer warriors across the country and around the world who were moved to pray for revival, and whose prayers were answered. Some people prominent in the River have, rightly or wrongly, been given a bad reputation in some circles. In most cases those things happened in later years. In quoting them I imply neither support nor non-support of anything they may have said or done outside the context of the citation.

In sum, the River revival sprang up spontaneously in answer to prayer, focused on worshipful sensitivity to God, and had thousands of people spending their free time in church and reading the Bible instead of walking the streets or watching television.

Characteristics of the River

As American streams of the River continued, the movement gradually shifted from an emphasis on God's power experienced in physical manifestations to an emphasis on God's presence experienced in a sense of divine love and even intimacy. Richard Crisco echoed a popular way of expressing this change of emphasis when he wrote,

> *In the recent past, the Church has done a lot of seeking; but much of that seeking has been for God's* hand, *and not for his face. Christians have sought the Lord only for what He could do for them and how He could bless them.*

The imagery sees God's hand as the source of blessings, what we can get God to do for us, whereas God's face represents an intimate personal relationship with God for love's sake. This new emphasis is illustrated in the opening words of a worship song written by Matthew Hardy and Ashley Thompson for the revival services at Baltimore's Rock City Church:

> *There was a time when I came to know your name.*
> *There have been times when I only sought your hand.*
> *But now, O Lord, I seek your face,*
> *For only your presence will do.*

According to Martyn Lloyd-Jones, author of *Revival*, this kind of emphasis is a sign of true revival.

> *It is indeed God coming down, God, as it were, no longer merely granting us the blessings. . . . It is a consciousness of the presence of God the Holy Spirit literally in the midst of the people.*

Several of the long-running River revivals began while guest speakers were preaching. This may be because people were hearing familiar truths expressed in a different way. Also, people often pay more attention to a "visiting expert" than their same old pastor. On the other hand, there is evidence in the Bible, revival history, and my own experience that some people seem to "carry an anointing" that can lead to revival whenever they visit a receptive place.

In some cases the guest speaker stayed on or returned to conduct most or all of the special revival services. In other places the pastor shared those duties with visiting evangelists or even pastors of nearby churches.

At Toronto and Brownsville, the revival services seem to have eclipsed the normal program of the churches, sometimes adding ministries, sometimes replacing them. At other churches, regular activities continued with the revival meetings added on.

Other characteristics common to the churches in the River include

- *An emphasis on prophetic intercession:* seeking God's guidance as to what to pray for, then praying for it fervently
- *A lack of focus on speaking in tongues and healing* compared to some previous revival movements; though both happened frequently, they were not central to the movement
- *A large role played by young children,* especially in giving prophetic messages and praying for healings
- *An interdenominational/nonsectarian flavor*
- *A lack of emphasis on any particular person* as leader
- *Evening services normally lasting several hours,* beginning with an extended time of musical worship and ending with a ministry time that continued until the last person had been ministered to
- *A belief that what was being experienced was the beginning* of a much greater revival, which may be the one that precedes the return of Christ.

Let me add here that I do not recall any kind of emphasis on money or offerings in any of the scores of River revival services I attended, with the exception of one traveling evangelist.

Every cultural phenomenon develops its own jargon, and the River was no different. Phrases commonly heard included

- *Soaking*: spending time resting receptively in the presence of God, often done in homes as part of individual or small-group worship
- *Carpet time:* lying on the floor, either as a voluntary prostration to pray or just rest in the presence of God, or as the result of having

been slain in the Spirit
- *Drunk in the Spirit* (Acts 2:13-16; Ephesians 5:18): when a person's mind and body were so joyfully overcome by the presence of God that the physical effect resembled a "happy drunk."

Differences of emphasis

Despite these similarities, the River movement was by no means monolithic. The Toronto revival, marked initially by laughter, was seen as primarily a revelation of the joy and grace of God, while people in the Brownsville revival typically found themselves weeping and feeling a call to repentance and holiness.

Randy Clark, John Arnott, and Rodney Howard-Browne saw "doing carpet time" as a valuable opportunity for God to minister within a person. On the other hand, I once heard Rick Joyner announce at a crowded conference, "Please don't fall on the floor. If you do we won't be responsible for what happens to you."

Some of the leaders in the River took various forms of corporate spiritual warfare very seriously, but in *How to Increase and Release the Anointing*, Howard-Browne wrote,

> *This game of spiritual warfare is nothing more than a spiritual Nintendo game played by baby Christians who have no understanding of the fact that Jesus defeated the devil two thousand years ago.*

Yet despite these differences, the overall attitude among the leaders of the different streams of the River was one of tolerance, humility, and mutual support. Randy Clark was typical when he wrote in *Learning How to Minister Under the Anointing*,

> *I caution you against turning my observations into laws . . . God uses other people in a way that is very different from what I have talked about, and it really is God. So don't make my observations and suggestions "Saul's armor."*

Criticism of the River

As with previous revivals, the River was called by some a "counterfeit revival" and "apostasy." These were not always malicious attacks. Church people trust their pastors to not let them be led astray. When a new spiritual movement surfaces, part of a pastor's job is to discern whether it is or is not of God, and then to lead their congregation either to embrace or avoid it. For pastors unfamiliar with revival, this placed them in a difficult position. Sometimes avoiding new things can seem like the safest course.

However, a revival is not a monolithic entity. Each service, each speaker, each member of the congregation introduces a different element. Each of these elements may involve a mixture of godly, human, and other influences. Thus the job of pastoring a revival is more complex than deciding whether to endorse or condemn an entire movement.

Almost all the religious criticism of the River revivals had to do with unusual behaviors reported to take place in some of the services. How to view these is a complicated question. We'll devote the next chapter to it.

3

Unusual Behaviors: Validation, Distraction, or Deception?

> *The house of the Lord was filled with a cloud, so that the priests could not stand to minister because of the cloud, for the glory of the Lord filled the house of God.*
> — 2 Chronicles 5:13–14 NAS

> *When He said to them, "I am He," they drew back and fell to the ground.*
> — John 18:6 NAS

> *An angel of the Lord descended from heaven and came and rolled away the stone and sat upon it. . . . The guards shook for fear of him and became like dead men.*
> — Matthew 28:2–4 NAS

As these verses demonstrate, human responses to a powerful manifestation of God's presence vary, but they can sometimes be dramatic.

Contemporary accounts of historical revivals, including the writings of such leaders as Jonathan Edwards, John Wesley, and Charles G. Finney, are replete with references to people trembling, crying out, falling to the ground, falling into trances, and even stranger occurrences. In fact, one can hardly find a major revival movement of the past in which such things did not happen — or which was not soundly castigated by many church leaders of the day because of them. Imagine if people started doing these things in one of your church services — especially if you were unprepared! This chapter is to make sure you won't be blindsided.

Unusual Behaviors Are Not New

Jonathan Edwards, in *A Faithful Narrative of the Surprising Work of God*, gives this account from the 1730s:

> *Their joyful surprise has caused their hearts as it were to leap, so that they have been ready to break forth into laughter, tears often at the same time issuing like a flood, and intermingling a loud weeping. Sometimes they have not been able to forbear crying out with a loud voice.*

At the famous Kentucky Cane Ridge camp meeting of August 1801, unusual behaviors were termed "exercises." Daniel Cohen writes in his book on revivalism in America,

> *The exercises came in six distinct varieties. They were commonly called the laughing and singing exercise, the falling exercise, the rolling exercise, the jerks, the barking exercise, and the dancing exercise.*

John Wesley, eighteenth-century founder of Methodism, often experienced physical reactions in his meetings. We'll look at his thoughts concerning them in the section on pastoral discernment and response.

As investment offers carefully remind us, past performance does not guarantee future results. As common as these behaviors were in recent revivals, they do not seem to have been a big part of what happened at Asbury and other colleges in 2023, though there were some isolated exceptions. Nonetheless, history implies at least the possibility that when the next revival comes, you as pastor may be called on to shepherd your people through what can be rather disconcerting events.

Objections

The most vociferous critics of unusual manifestations seem to be those who've had the least experience with them. Their objections are usually for one of three reasons:

1. Some believe that miracles, prophetic gifts, and anything else that can't be explained by natural causes and scientific reasoning are superstitious or magical thinking and do not really exist (anti-supernaturalist theology).
2. Others acknowledge that God worked in miraculous or supernatural ways in Bible times, but believe he ceased working that way after the Bible was completed and the twelve apostles died (cessationist theology).
3. Still others feel that some behaviors violate Paul's direction that *all things should be done decently and in order* (1 Corinthians 14:40 ESV).

Validation, Distraction, or Deception?

Proponents of unusual behaviors often see them as validation, manifestations of God's presence that prove God is working in the revival. Others see them as purely human distractions. Some critics even consider them a demonic deception.

Properly discerning the source of these behaviors is at the heart of your pastoral responsibility. Let's look at the possibilities more closely.

Divine validation

Proponents claim unusual behaviors in revival services are manifestations of God's presence and power that validate the revival as a true move of God. In addition to the verses cited at the beginning of this chapter, they point to passages like these:

- *You will receive power when the Holy Spirit comes upon you.* (Acts 1:8 NLT)
- *My speech and my message were not in plausible words of wisdom, but in demonstration of the Spirit and of power, so that your faith might not rest in the wisdom of men but in the power of God.* (1 Corinthians 2:4–5 ESV)
- *The kingdom of God does not consist in talk but in power.* (1 Corinthians 4:20 ESV)
- *. . . having a form of godliness but denying its power. Have nothing to do with such people.* (2 Timothy 3:5 NIV)
- *Very truly I tell you, whoever believes in me will do the works I have been doing, and they will do even greater things than these, because I am going to the Father.* (John 14:12 NIV)

Certainly, God can move without a visible demonstration of divine power, but people cannot move in divine power without God. If truly divine power is demonstrated, clearly God must be present.

Human distraction

There's no question that people crying out, moving oddly, and falling on the floor can be distracting. Some critics argue that God would not cause such distractions from the proper business of a worship service, which they see as praising God, proclaiming the gospel, and administering the sacraments.

Most in this category attribute unusual behaviors to human emotionalism, responses to psychological suggestions from the leader, or an unconscious desire to fit in by doing what others are doing. Some go further and accuse revival leaders of deliberate emotional manipulation. Others believe the manifestations are completely fraudulent, engaged in by henchmen of the revivalist to excite people and gain notoriety for the leader.

Demonic deception

The third explanation advanced for unusual behaviors is that those engaging in them are being spiritually deceived, and the behaviors are actually demonic in origin.

Many in the secular world, and even many pastors, would dismiss this explanation out of hand as ignorant superstition or, at the least, based on an unwarrantedly literal interpretation of scripture. However, it has been said that Satan's greatest deception is making us believe that he does not exist. Ironically, this can be exacerbated by those who claim that anything they disagree with is demonic.

Well-attested experience throughout revival history indicates that some strange behaviors may indeed be demonic in origin. These can be demonically inspired actions aimed at causing a distraction or throwing doubt on the validity of what God was doing. More often they were the reactions of demons to a powerful presence of God, as in Mark 9:25-26, where a demon threw a boy to the ground in the presence of Jesus.

Demonic manifestations can be common where God is moving. Claudio Freidzon, a leading pastor in the Argentine revival, recalls his early experiences in *Holy Spirit, I Hunger for You*. "Dozens of men and women gave indications of being demon-possessed, and we had to deal with them in a separate place." Many pastors have found the best thing to do in those cases is to move the afflicted people to where they will not disturb the flow of the meeting, and have a specially trained team of deliverance ministers work with them. In fact, this is a good way to deal with anyone who is disrupting the meeting in a negative way, demonic or not.

Demonic influence should be a diagnosis of last resort, and deliverance ministry should be left to those called to it. However, if you are forced to deal with a situation of possible demonic influence, take the authority Jesus gave. In the Great Commission, Jesus commanded the apostles to *make disciples . . . teaching them to observe all that I have commanded you* (Matthew 28:19–20 ESV). One of the things Jesus commanded was to cast out demons (Matthew 10:8). We see this demonstrated years later in the ministry of Philip, who was not one of the twelve apostles (Acts 8:7). Mentions of this authority can be seen throughout church history.

If you are not familiar with deliverance ministry, I encourage you to learn about it. Begin with your own Bible study on the subject. Books many have found helpful include *The X-Manual: Exousia—A Comprehensive Handbook on Deliverance and Exorcism*, by seminary professors Peter J. Bellini and Stephen A. Seamands; *Biblical Guide to Deliverance*, by Randy Clark; and *Free in Christ*, by Argentine deliverance minister Pablo Bottari. If you feel called to go further, the surest way is to find a mature Christian experienced in this area and learn from them in person.

My View: It's Complicated

Why do these physical manifestations happen, and why do they differ from person to person and revival to revival?

Much of it, of course, depends on what God is doing in a given situation. But the human element plays a bigger part than many might suppose.

I like to believe that every sermon and worship song I wrote over thirty-eight years of ministry started from divine inspiration transmitted through my human spirit. But I also know that each one had to work its way through my human mind and my physical voice, with very uneven results. Sometimes I took the time to really hear God, sometimes I was rushed. Sometimes I felt good, sometimes I felt bad. Sometimes I lost my train of thought or fumbled a guitar chord.

God has chosen to work through people. The fact that a message, song, or other activity is inspired or initiated by God doesn't guarantee that it is perfectly delivered by the human vessel through whom it is given. And the fact that it is imperfectly delivered does not invalidate the inspiration of the message.

Different people can respond to the same spiritual stimulus in very different ways. I remember one time when a person going out of church thanked me for something they thought I said in my sermon, and the person right behind them thanked me because they thought they heard the exact opposite! As a pastor, you've probably had similar experiences.

Different and even inappropriate responses to a move of God do not mean it was not really God. Most people's responses to almost anything are filtered through their personality, their experiences, their current circumstances, and what they've been taught.

For instance, I was in a small-town ecumenical worship service a few years ago when the leader called everyone to a time of prayer. Some came up to the altar; some stood where they were with hands raised and head up; some knelt in the pew with hands folded and heads bowed, facing toward the front; some sat; some turned around and knelt with their hands folded over the pew seats. Some prayed silently, some prayed quietly in English, some prayed in tongues. All were sincerely responding to the move of the Holy Spirit. No way of responding was better or worse than any other. But almost every person did it the way they had learned in their church. Does that mean it wasn't really God? Does it mean one way was of God and the rest were merely human? Of course not.

The same dynamic holds with responses to a sense of God's presence in revival. Those who were active in a previous move of God are used to the responses of that time. Very naturally, they will tend to respond the same way to the next move. It may be that their actions are genuinely Spirit-led. It may also be that they learned thirty years ago that a certain action is what you're supposed to do in a revival. Just because it's a learned behavior doesn't mean it is wrong or inappropriate.

On the other hand, in the new thing God is doing, some of the old responses might be more of a distraction than a blessing, especially if the old veterans attempt to "correct" what happens in the new move.

The point is, discerning whether God is present in a revival service or movement is not an either-or, all-or-nothing proposition. God does not make us puppets. Our response to what God is doing is subject to our own humanness, with all the mix of psychological, physical, and cultural influences that implies. Not just the overall movement, but every part of it, calls for careful pastoral discernment.

Here's the way I understand it. God created human beings in God's image (Genesis 1:26-27). As God is the inseparable divine Trinity of Father, Son, and Holy Spirit, he created us as an inseparable human trinity of spirit, soul, and body (1 Thessalonians 5:23).

Have you ever tried to think analytically when you had the flu, or pray fervently on two hours of sleep? Have you ever not noticed a physical injury in the excitement of playing sports, or let the intellectual stimulation of tracking down the particular meaning of a Bible verse distract you from its spiritual message? Each part of our being affects every other part.

Among other things, that means our ability to receive, interpret, respond to, and apply what God tells us or gives us is partial. The portion of our human spirit that is truly in tune with God is not the only factor. Our personality, physical condition, expectations, mood, worries, and many other factors also enter into how we interpret and respond to a move of God's Spirit. I'm sure that many times the spiritual impact of one of my sermons was cut short because someone was worried about the roast in their oven!

This truth has direct and specific application to what we do in church. In fact, Paul thought it was important enough to mention its implications three times in the section of his writings that most directly addresses the conduct of public worship.

- *We know in part and we prophesy in part* (1 Corinthians 13:9 ESV)
- *Let two or three people prophesy, and let the others evaluate what is said* (1 Corinthians 14:29 NLT)
- *The spirits of prophets are subject to prophets* (1 Corinthians 14:32 ESV).

Paul is saying that even when things originate directly from God, like prophecy, we humans have an amazing ability to get at least part of it wrong. The appropriate response is not judgment but collaboration.

The fact that elements of personality or learned behavior may be discernible in a person's response to a move of God in no way lessens the genuineness of the experience. As pastor, receive and encourage what you discern to be from God. At the same time, don't hesitate to give guidance where a human element may be mixed in. You don't need to worry about quenching the Holy Spirit in another person if your correction is guided by the Holy Spirit in you.

Every situation will be different. Have confidence in your discernment of God's leading and your understanding of the dynamics involved.

Pastoral Discernment and Response

Worship, prayer, confession, and physical actions such as trembling, weeping, laughing, and falling down are common responses to a powerful presence of the Holy Spirit. The particular form they take for each person is influenced not only by what God wants to do in them, but also by a mix of each individual's spiritual, mental, emotional, and physical state, their personality type, and their expectations, based on what they have seen or heard of previous moves of God, what they are told by the speaker, and what they see others doing.

This mixed response is one factor that makes pastoring revival so difficult. What is the proper pastoral approach to these phenomena?

The first task is to discern the source. Is it the response of a human body overcome by the power of God? Is it a human imitation of such a response? Is it the response of a demonic presence within the person reacting to the presence of God? Or could it be a combination of these?

As pastor, whenever you are not the one preaching or conducting a service, you have two main responsibilities. First, guard your people against false teaching and things that would draw them away from God. Second, see that everything is done decently and in order (1

Corinthians 14:40).

Of course, what is considered decent and orderly in a Pentecostal service may seem chaotic to a Presbyterian. So part of your discernment is to consider whether a given activity is outside the bounds of decent Biblical order, or just outside the bounds of your own comfort zone.

How do we discern between what the Holy Spirit inspires and what is merely learned or cultural behavior? While there is no obvious answer to such questions, we must beware of creating a false dichotomy.

Don't assume that a learned or cultural behavior cannot be inspired by God. If a way of doing something, whether it be taking the offering or dancing in the Spirit, is basically the same after revival as before, it may indicate a cultural or learned aspect to that element of worship, but that does not necessarily imply that the Holy Spirit is not in it.

Perhaps one of the key requirements for pastoring ongoing revival is the willingness to live with such questions rather than seeking to analyze and pigeonhole everything. The temptation to strictly label things as either "of the Spirit" or "not of the Spirit" might well be a contributing factor to the death of some revivals. Proper spiritual discernment is a clear biblical duty for all Christians, and especially pastors. Putting God in a box, however, is one of the fastest ways to grieve and quench his ever-dynamic, ever-creative Spirit.

As mentioned earlier, John Wesley was no stranger to unusual behaviors in his meetings. He spent much time thinking and praying about them, and recorded his ponderings in his journal.

> *I look upon some of those bodily symptoms to have been preternatural or diabolical, and others to have been effects which in some circumstances naturally followed from strong and sudden emotions of mind. Those emotions of mind, whether of fear, sorrow, or joy, I believe were chiefly supernatural, springing from the*

gracious influences of the Spirit of God which accompanied his word.

Wesley saw the pattern as follows:

1. God suddenly and strongly convinced many they were lost sinners, the natural consequence whereof were sudden outcries and bodily convulsions; 2. To strengthen and encourage them that believed, and to make his work more apparent, he favored several of them with divine dreams, often with trances and visions; 3. In some of these instances, after a time, nature mixed with grace; 4. Satan likewise mimicked this work of God, in order to discredit the whole. . . . At first it was doubtless, wholly from God. It is partly so at this day; and he will enable us to discern how far in every case the work is pure, and where it mixes and degenerates.

In Brownsville, Pastor John Kilpatrick developed a list of five questions to help in discerning whether a particular activity was of God. He trained his altar workers and ushers to use these same questions to maintain order.

1. Is Jesus being lifted up?
2. Is this creating a greater hunger for God and His Word?
3. Is this leading people to love God and each other more?
4. Is this bringing truth and greater spiritual depth?
5. Is there any practical change taking place (sometimes this must be judged over a period of time)?

Roger Helland, in *Let the River Flow*, provides and comments on a similar list of criteria for judging the phenomena, based on the writings of Jonathan Edwards:

UNUSUAL BEHAVIORS: VALIDATION, DISTRACTION, OR DECEPTION?

1. Does it esteem the Lord Jesus Christ?
2. Does it operate against the interests of Satan's kingdom?
3. Does it honor the Scriptures?
4. Does it operate as a spirit of truth?
5. Does it operate as a spirit of love for God and people?

John Wesley advised his followers to test the manifestations.

> *I warned them, all these [manifestations] were in themselves, of a doubtful, disputable, nature; they might be from God, and they might not; and were simply not to be relied on, (any more than simply to be condemned,) but . . . to be brought to the only certain test, the Law and the Testimony.*

Wesley stressed that a changed life is the only sure sign of God working.

> *I know several persons in whom this great change was wrought in a dream . . . And that such a change was then wrought, appears (not from their shedding tears only, or falling into fits, or crying out: These are not the fruits, as you seem to suppose, whereby I judge, but) from the whole tenor of their life, till then, many ways wicked; from that time, holy, just, and good.*

Given the ambivalent nature of physical manifestations, what should be the pastoral approach to them? In 1759 Wesley provided good balance as he looked back at the early days of the Methodist revival:

> *The danger <u>was</u>, to regard extraordinary circumstances too much, such as outcries, convulsions, visions, trances; as if these were essential to the inward work. . . . Perhaps the danger <u>is</u> to regard them too little, to condemn them altogether, to imagine they had*

nothing of God in them, and were a hindrance to his work.

Differences of Experience

So far we've been talking about those who experience manifestations of different kinds. In every meeting, however, there will be others who do not experience anything. This difference immediately raises concerns in a pastor's heart. How do we minister to these disparate experiences? Roger Helland sensitively writes,

> *There must be wisdom to pastor the phenomena. God loves everyone, and works in a unique way with each person. Even though we may teach this, some won't believe it. "That person was touched, why wasn't I?" They will need assurance. . . . Because the gifts of God are based on grace and not on merit, they appear to be unfair. . . . Therefore, people must be taught not to strive or unrealistically expect things to happen to them. Yes, they should seek the gifts and grace of God; they should be open to receive, but they should not set themselves up for disappointment or failure. . . . We must give gentle counsel and not fail to use models and testimonies of people who have renewal fruit but did* not *experience dramatic manifestations.*

Whatever the cause, the guiding principle is found in Jesus' parable of the tares and the wheat in Matthew 13. In a 1998 academic paper, seminary professor Steve Seamands quoted Francis Asbury, contemporary and colleague of John Wesley:

> *The friends of order may allow a guilty mortal to tremble at God's word . . . and the saints to cry and shout when the Holy One of Israel is in the midst of them. To be hasty in plucking up the tares,*

is to endanger the wheat.

Seamands went on to comment,

> There were many in Wesley's day who accused him of being an enthusiast [fanatic] because he let so many tares remain. There are many today who would say the same thing about those who are pastoring what's going on in Toronto. My point is that when you function with this more complex understanding of the sources of manifestations, you sometimes may allow some tares among the wheat. At other times you may determine that the tares are indeed taking over and they've got to be plucked out for the sake of the wheat.

In other words, sometimes you have to let some less desirable things happen, to avoid the collateral damage of accidentally shutting down genuine new experiences.

Slain in the Spirit

The most characteristic physical manifestation of recent revivals, with the possible exception of weeping, is being "slain in the Spirit." This term, and others such as "falling under the power" and "doing carpet time," refer to a person falling to the ground, purportedly under the influence of the Holy Spirit. Sometimes it happens when a revival leader touches them on the forehead, giving rise to the charge by critics that those who fall were actually pushed, but often there is no physical contact at all. Looking at the way different leaders in the River movement dealt with this phenomenon can help us as we prayerfully consider how we will respond if unusual behaviors come to our churches.

Martyn Lloyd-Jones, author of *Revival*, explains it this way:

> *Sometimes this sense of power and glory is so great that people are prostrated to the ground by reason of it. As you hear of people literally fainting when they suddenly get a piece of good news, which they have not expected, so, when men and women experience this glorious presence, sometimes, it is too much for the physical frame.*

An excellent treatment of this subject is Francis MacNutt's *Overcome by the Spirit*. One chapter lists the following positive results of the experience:

- A demonstration of God's power
- An intimate experience of God's presence
- An impetus to conversion or repentance
- An environment for healing
- Healing of body and spirit—including physical healing, inner healing, and deliverance from evil spirits

In revivals where this phenomenon often happens, pastors and leaders usually provide "catchers." These are people trained to stand behind those they believe might fall, to ease them to the ground. (For some reason, those slain in the Spirit almost never fall forwards.)

There was friendly disagreement among revival leaders over the question of whether the possibility of falling in the Spirit should be mentioned as people were being invited to ministry time. Some were concerned that talking about it could create a psychological suggestion in some people's minds, resulting in people falling because they felt it was expected. Francis MacNutt, while acknowledging this possibility, opted to briefly explain the phenomenon so first-time visitors would not panic if people started falling down around them. He wrote in *Overcome by the Spirit*,

> *I try first to give the purposes of resting in the Spirit as I see them, and then — to obviate the power of suggestion as much as possible — I ask people neither to seek the phenomenon nor to fight it. If we manufacture it, no one is helped. Indeed, trying to make it happen can actually block anything God might wish to do.*

It's important, when discussing this phenomenon, not to raise expectations too high. True, it sometimes happens to people who are resisting falling or even skeptical about its reality — including one of my own teenage sons during a visit to the Toronto Airport Christian Fellowship. More often, though, those who experience it have responded to an invitation for prayer and have seen others fall to the ground before them.

The slain in the Spirit phenomenon is nuanced over a continuum of experiences, from those who voluntarily prostrate themselves in adoration, to those who come expecting to fall, to those who fall despite their efforts to remain standing. Neither end of this continuum is more or less spiritual than the other. The attitude of the body does not necessarily reflect the attitude of the heart.

II

Part 2: Three Case Studies

Now these things happened to them as an example, but they were written down for our instruction, on whom the end of the ages has come.
— *1 Corinthians 10:11 ESV*

4

Case Study 1: Rock City Church of Baltimore

I first became aware of the revival at Rock City Church in late 1997, when my wife Paula found accounts of it on the internet. What I experienced there had a lasting impact on my life and ministry.

Rock City Church is a non-denominational church situated on a hill just off an intersection of the Baltimore Beltway (Interstate 695). It sprang out of Rock Church of Virginia Beach, Virginia, one of the first large charismatic churches on the East Coast. I chose it as one of my dissertation case studies for three reasons.

- Compared to the movements in Toronto and Pensacola, the outpouring in Baltimore reflected a greater emphasis on intimately experiencing God's presence. This was in character with what seemed to be the most recent focus in the move of God.
- The location, about 45 minutes away from my church in Maryland, was convenient.
- Most importantly, I felt that the revival at Rock City Church might be the beginning of a regional revival that could involve the church I pastored.

Beginnings

In 1983 Bart Pierce, a former professional surfer and building contractor, moved from Virginia with his wife Coralee to pastor a struggling church of thirty-eight people meeting in a tent on the north side of Baltimore, Maryland. Less than a year later there were five hundred people in the church. By 1993 the church numbered 1,500.

Then Pierce took a year off to investigate other ministry possibilities. His return met with great misunderstanding and confusion. By 1995, when the church moved into the present three-thousand-seat sanctuary, attendance had dropped back to five or six hundred. It stayed in that range for the next year.

Though technically located in the suburbs, Rock City Church was and remains an intentionally multi-ethnic congregation with a focus on ministering to the city of Baltimore, especially the poor. This was seen not only through traditional programs such as a food pantry but also in more unexpected ways. For instance, if an inner-city child was killed in a drug deal or gang fight and the family or local church could not afford to buy a coffin, Rock City Church would often quietly pay the bill. During the course of my study, in fact, the church changed its name from Rock Church to Rock City Church (now Rock City Church of Baltimore) in order to emphasize its focus on the needs of the city.

In mid-January, 1997, Pierce attended a pastor's retreat in Florida where he met evangelist Tommy Tenney. He invited Tenney to accompany him back to Baltimore to speak. Pierce described the eighteen-hour drive north as "an encounter with God as we talked about what God was doing and what we believed."

When they arrived at the church the next morning, Sunday, January 17th, they found two elders standing inside the door weeping, just as the Pierces and Tenney had wept during the drive. When worship started, people began crying out and falling under the power of God throughout the building.

That Sunday morning service lasted until 2:00 a.m. Monday. Revival had begun.

Tenney, who lived in Louisiana, preached revival services in the Baltimore church almost every Monday and Tuesday evening for more than four years, while traveling internationally for preaching engagements during the rest of the week. Pierce and Tenney grew so close that when I interviewed them together they often finished each other's sentences. During this time, Tenney wrote his first books, *The God Chasers*, *God's Dream Team*, and *God's Favorite House*.

The Baltimore revival did not receive as much media attention as Toronto or Pensacola, but word got out, especially via a July 1998 feature article in *Charisma* magazine. People came from across the nation and around the world.

Bart Pierce already had some experience with the press. In 1988 Baltimore Orioles star pitcher Scott McGregor gave up baseball to become an assistant pastor at Rock City Church. Pierce resisted the temptation to use the situation for publicity, choosing rather to shield McGregor as he matured in the faith. Pierce demonstrated the same attitude toward the revival.

I attended worship services at Rock City Church a dozen or more times between 1997 and 2000. All but two of these visits were to the Monday or Tuesday evening revival services. In the course of gathering data for my dissertation, I also visited a complete Sunday morning service, which stretched well into the afternoon. In addition, I attended two internationally advertised teaching conferences held at Rock City Church, and traveled there three times for interviews. One of these interview occasions occurred on a Sunday evening and I was able to experience the beginning of a regular Sunday evening service.

The revival at Rock City Church was characterized by a quiet intimacy with the Holy Spirit. The phenomena associated with other outbreaks of the River were not unknown at Rock City Church, but they were not the focus. The attitude was one of seeking the loving presence of God, and then allowing God to do whatever he wanted to do. The worship music, much of it composed in-house, was written and performed with a becoming combination of skill and humility. Tenney's preaching was gentle and engaging. Either alone was worth the effort to get to the services. But it was clear that the sole purpose of both music and preaching was to usher in the presence of the Holy Spirit. Indeed, Tenney often spent more time inviting people to experience God's presence and love than he did preaching.

Unlike at some revivals, Tenney did not line people up and lay hands on them all himself. He did join Pierce and other pastors and prayer counselors in individually praying for people during the end-of-service ministry time, but he preferred to encourage people to open themselves to the Holy Spirit right where they were rather than seeking prayer from a particular person. As a result, at the end of the service people would be found quietly weeping, rejoicing, praising, and receiving from God all over the sanctuary.

Seven Characteristics

The revival at Rock City Church was marked by seven characteristics.

1. An emphasis on worship
2. A strong sense of God's presence
3. Lasting personal transformation
4. A lack of self-promotion on the part of the leaders
5. A marked devotion to the revival services on the part of many members of the congregation
6. An intentional and successful effort to involve pastors and people of other churches

7. Increased motivation and power in social ministries.

An emphasis on worship

If one word defined the revival at Rock City Church, it was worship. The emphasis was constantly on seeking a greater closeness of God for God's own sake. The phrase often used was, "seek his face, not his hand"—that is, seek to know God for who God is, rather than for what he can do for us.

The Monday and Tuesday revival services began at 7:00pm with worship music. After an hour or so, Tommy Tenney would quietly begin encouraging people to enter God's presence. It was often hard to tell when he transitioned from that to preaching, or if he transitioned at all.

Instead of a plea for contributions, people brought their offerings to the front while the singing continued. There were usually no announcements and no introductions. Pastor Pierce was always there, but often an entire service would go by without him ever taking the microphone.

Sometimes there was a call for people to come to the front for special prayer, sometimes there was not. Repentance, healing, re-dedication, and other spiritual transactions were sometimes mentioned, but more often, they were implicitly expected to happen as a result of the Holy Spirit working within people.

At various times through the service, a significant percentage of the congregation could be found prostrated in prayer—sometimes at the front of the auditorium, sometimes in the aisles, sometimes under the pews.

There was usually no official end to the service. People left when they finished their business with God, often not until 11:00 p.m. or later. Usually the gifted pianist and singer-songwriter, Ashley Thompson, had been playing and worshipping nonstop since the service began. Often the whole praise team were involved for much of that time as well.

The Sunday morning service I attended was very similar to the evening revival services, though more structured. It lasted about four hours, which the large congregation did not seem to think was an unusual amount of time to spend in worship.

The attitude was perhaps best expressed by layperson Kay Culver, who told me, "We just come in and say, 'God, what can we do for you tonight? What kind of mood are you in?' And our hearts are always broken, always ready for him to do whatever he wants to do."

As in most churches, a key vehicle for expressing worship was music. Tenney called music "the cradle in which the baby of worship is carried." He felt music should make worship easy. Revival is possible with hymns and traditional songs; they can be wells of the water of revival. But tradition tends to produce comfort, which dulls the spiritual hunger so necessary for revival. The key is music, whether contemporary or traditional, that reflects what God is doing and wants to do in the people.

Music minister Don Mark told me, "Before this [revival] started we were singing songs that made us feel good—songs about us—without a whole lot of consideration about ministering to the Lord. We're now singing songs about mercy and about love—songs of passion, songs of our heart."

Mark is an accomplished musician leading a quality worship team, but he no longer carefully scripts the worship service. "I pretty much come in here with an idea, after having prayed, where the service may go, then I listen from song to song for the Holy Spirit to lead me."

Almost all the worship music used in the revival services was written at Rock City Church. Fifteen or more different people at the church wrote scores of songs. As Mark put it, "We are hearing God's words and we have placed them to music." Tenney explained, "When God visits, there are new songs and they'll take you on to the next little piece."

Mark summed up, "We consider our worship to be vertical. We come in here to minister to the heart of God. If we delight the Lord, then we've accomplished something we're trying to do in each service."

A sense of God's presence

The second major characteristic of the revival at Rock City Church was a pervasive intense sense of the presence of God. It was often described as something almost tangible. Gwynn Hill, director of the Hiding Place, the church's home for women in crisis pregnancy, told me that when the residents were brought to the revival services, "They come right into this and experience what God is doing."

The sense of God's presence was not limited to adults. According to Kay Culver, "All our kids have experienced it. One time we had so many kids come that just got blasted out in the Holy Spirit that we just had to open the doors and bring them out in the hallway and pray on them. We'd never had this before, even three-, four-, five-year-olds just getting into the worship and everything." She added, "Pastor and Brother Tommy have emphasized that it's not the size of the crowd; it's not who does or doesn't come; it's that the presence of God is here."

But the crowd was usually sizeable. One member explained it very simply: "God's presence was so strong here, people just began to gravitate."

The sense of God's presence was not limited to the church sanctuary. Staff pastor Bob Martak related a common experience when he said, "I've been in my home, and in my car, and I lose control of all my emotions because God's presence, when it comes upon me, it's just like his arms are wrapped around me. There's never been a feeling that's as wonderful or as powerful as that feeling is."

Lasting personal transformation

A recurring theme, especially among the laypeople interviewed, was the personal transformation that came about in their lives since the revival began.

Kay Culver described her experience this way: "You think you're saved until God comes a little bit closer and then you realize how much more you need to change. God has turned a lot of my focus into getting rid of the selfishness and to look at the real depth of my heart and the depth of my purpose and motives for everything that I do. It has totally transformed the way I see things. God has given me boldness in a lot of areas. I'm now dancing where I was scared to death to show any kind of worship or freedom or expression of love. Our hearts have not been the same. Even my job has been impacted by what's happened here because I've changed."

Staff pastor K. C. Carter, director of Adopt-a-Block and A Can Can Make a Difference ministries, related, "I was here before the revival broke out, and was being raised up in that ministry where I was just running in the flesh, thinking I was doing something. After the revival fell there was a big change in my life. I began to repent every day. I learned that I should be obedient to God's word, what I was hearing through the Spirit, what I was hearing by my spiritual authority."

Music minister Don Mark echoed those sentiments. "When his presence came in such a dynamic way, I found out how far away from God I really was. I thought I was in God. I wasn't even close. So there is this tremendous repentance that takes place."

Member Pam Pauley said, "When this first started, my heart was hard. He just broke my heart and I began to cry and weep, and ever since then it's like I can't stop it! A gift of intercession came out that

I'd never had before."

In the culture of Rock City Church being broken is a good thing, implying openness to God. In fact, it's something to be sought and protected, not only for the individual's sake, but for the sake of maintaining revival in the church as a whole. Member Gwynn Hill put it this way: "One of the things that I've learned is to maintain a brokenness, a broken heart, a repentant heart, a clean heart, a guarded heart. To stay guarded with what's going to protect what God is doing here and not to allow gaps and a major breaking down where the enemy can come in."

Pierce explained, "The more you get in this, the more I find people who are in sin and never knew it. It starts getting exposed. Your whole moral compass starts to line up with God's compass. Years and years of church life will put so much debris in our heart that we can't even hear God, we can't even find God, though we are sitting in a place with his name smeared all over it. Repentance opens again that heart for removal of the debris. Once we get the debris out of our lives, then we can go into the world and know his glory's going to come."

Pastor Carter summarized, "There are churches that are going to hell in a bobsled. If you ask people in the churches, they're miserable. All we did, we fell back in love with our God. When you are in love, you don't mind showing off. You don't mind walking down the street with a glory. We just fell back in love with our heavenly Father. If this isn't God, I'd rather do this until he comes."

Lack of self-promotion

Many people think of revival like Neil Diamond's song, "Brother Love's Traveling Salvation Show," with all the focus on a charismatic personality on the stage. That was decidedly not the case at Rock City Church. Sometimes an entire revival service would pass without Pierce ever taking the microphone. In fact, it was not until I had attended several revival services that I was even sure who the pastor was.

Church member Kay Culver observed, "Pastor Bart just humbles himself to allow God to do what he wants to do, and he gives God the place. He steps down. I've watched him almost in a physical motion, just step back and say, 'Okay, God.' He and Brother Tommy both do that. It's like, whatever God wants to do."

This attitude carried over into the approach toward physical manifestations. As we've seen, some revival leaders sought to prepare people for manifestations or even play them up, leading critics to say they were merely responses to psychological suggestion. Pierce told me, "What I've chosen to do simply is not prepare them, because I couldn't get the balance [between preparation and suggestion]."

Instead, Pierce addressed unusual behavior after it happened, if he addressed it at all. He prepared a flyer with Bible references to give to people who questioned what they saw or experienced. As for Tenney, he felt that kind of decision belonged to the pastor. "I don't ever even touch it, because that's not my place as the evangelist."

I saw a similar attitude in other areas. Personal prophecy, in which a person feels they have received a specific message from God for an individual rather than a general word for the congregation, was acknowledged as a gift of God, but it was not emphasized. Even sermons, while carefully prepared, were not the centerpiece of the service. Pierce and Tenney felt the presence of God spoke more directly to people's needs than any sermon could.

This attitude of humility carried over to the rest of the church. Layperson Wayman Hicks related, "In one of the meetings Tommy Tenney and Pastor Bart preached about how revival should affect you in such a way that you really do become a servant. That's the thing I see in a lot of people's lives, they come and become more of a servant. I was asked to become an usher. There was shift in my experience of revival at that point."

A member of the staff expressed the common view. "God has a thing to do. We are here to give God a place to do that, to give people a place to come. It may be that he will do that at other places, but for right now it seems to be that he wants to do it here. We are just helping to facilitate it."

Devotion to the revival services

The revival at Rock City Church sparked a remarkable devotion among many people. A number of the laypeople I interviewed claimed to have been at every service since they started coming. Ashley Thompson, the unpaid pianist whose voice and music defined the Rock City revival almost as much as Tommy Tenney's preaching, was at work from the beginning to the end of every service since the start of the revival, except for a brief absence to give birth.

Usher Hicks admitted there was a cost to such devotion. "For the first year and a half, my wife and I both attended revival services. We have two little kids, and for the majority of the time I was just on the floor, bawling [in response to God's presence], while my wife did stuff with the kids. So, after that year and a half, we made an agreement that she would come on Mondays and I would watch the kids, and I would come Tuesdays and she would watch the kids. A number of us have paid the cost—my wife and I, my family. But I guess what we've gotten from it has outweighed any sacrifice. The things we've given up, we've decided we can do without."

Perhaps the record for effort to attend belonged to Ruth Cave and her husband Bob: "We travel an hour and forty minutes every service to get here. We live in New Jersey. We come down at least twice a week. When they have special meetings, conferences, Sunday mornings, we're here for all that also." The reason? "It has changed my life."

Such devotion was not due to threats or cajoling from the pulpit. Michael James Allen, a faithful attender, declared, "Every time we're here at these revival services, we're here because we want to be here."

Many people came from distant places to experience what God was doing. Church secretary Ciel Grammar told me, "We see so many people coming in from other states and countries and we see how they are being touched and they are being blessed. It's so neat to see them coming to the altar, sitting in the pews crying, pouring their hearts out, and they don't know us. They just know God is here. They are just so touched to be here."

The multicultural membership of Rock City Church combined with the international visitors to create tremendous diversity. Member Michael James Allen commented, "I have never been in a church where I saw so many different ethnic groups come together. At a service one night, there were twenty-four different nationalities here."

Hicks added, "As ushers, it gives us an opportunity to ask, 'Why are you coming here? Why from so far away?' The main theme is that these folks are just so desperate for God, and where they are attending church, they don't experience it. They are willing to sacrifice, pay the cost. Tuesday night when I come in, I always take a count for myself. Seventy to eighty percent of the people that come are not members here. Out of that seventy to eighty percent, thirty or forty percent are new for the first time."

Sharing with other churches

In all the services I attended, I never once heard anything that could be construed as an attempt to woo members away from other churches. Pierce's vision was for people in other parts of the world to say, "I'm going to the revival in Baltimore," and when asked what church, to be able to say, "I hear it doesn't matter, it's in all of them." He believed, "It has to go outside of this church. If it doesn't go outside of this church, it will not be what [God's] plan is to touch the city, the nation, and the world."

Pierce has been instrumental in bringing the pastors of the greater Baltimore area together, promoting the idea that they are not the pastors of their individual congregations as much as co-pastors of the city.

In February 1998, Rock City Church sponsored a three-day "Peace for the City" retreat attended by approximately sixty pastors from a variety of denominations and non-denominational churches in the Baltimore area. The focus was on prayer for unity and revival in greater Baltimore. Bart Pierce, taking a typically low-key, behind-the-scenes approach, invited others to do the preaching. The retreat was repeated in 1999, and again in 2000. I was blessed to attend all three.

The Baltimore Covenant, which codified the idea that all the ministers of a city co-pastor it together, was drawn up at the first of these. Pierce and Tenney, supplying words for each other's thoughts, said of the covenant, "It didn't create unity, but it created the boundaries, the road for unity to come."

The Baltimore Covenant

> *We, the city-wide Gatekeepers, covenant this day to submit to the commandment of our Lord Jesus Christ reflected in John 13:34,35 that we will be known by our love one to another. "A new commandment I give unto you, that ye love one another; as I have loved you, that ye also love one another. By this shall all men know that ye are my disciples, if ye have love one to another."*
>
> *We purpose in our heart to fulfill the call to oneness as expressed in Ephesians 4:1-6 by these actions:*

- *We covenant in sharing of pulpits without regard to race, ethnic, national origin, or denominational affiliation.*
- *We covenant that in securing our city-wide borders as Gatekeepers, we will not allow schism, disputes, unkind criticism, or defamation of character in our midst.*
- *We covenant as fellow shepherds and brethren in the Messiah, we will not tolerate the unethical practice of sheep stealing and recycling of disgruntled members without conferring one with another. We agree that these matters will be handled in the spirit of reconciliation.*
- *We covenant to deal with a fallen brother or sister in love according to Biblical principles as stated in Galatians 6:1. "Brethren, if a man be overtaken in a fault, ye which are spiritual, restore such an one in the spirit of meekness; considering thyself, lest thou also be tempted."*
- *We consciously covenant to fellowship together, covering one another in the spirit of prayer, protection, and care.*

As we covenant to pastor our city, we commit our gifts, callings and resources to our brethren to strengthen the work of the Kingdom, for a great "Harvest of Souls."

I, _____, as a Gatekeeper, sign this covenant in commitment to the articles above herein stated.

Usher Wayman Hicks observed, "There are no differences, we're all pastoring the city. To see these pastors come in here and hug and put their differences aside, only the true presence of God could do these things."

Kay Culver added, "That's the thing us women noticed. Men were touched during this revival, men were crying, men were coming together. Male pastors were coming together, as well as some female pastors in this city. Pastor Bart Pierce's heart is to gather the pastors together because he knows the power of that unity against the enemy and for the advancement of the Kingdom of God."

One staff pastor said, "We're starting to network with churches that we've never had a relationship with before. That signals a paradigm shift. We're just along for the ride."

Hicks sounded like he was paraphrasing John Wesley as he summed up. "Pastor is always looking to unify in everything. I think it's one of the reasons why God has really blessed him to see such great things in the church here. Pastor doesn't squabble over doctrine. He taught that to us. Bottom line is: Is your heart right with God? Are you right in your relationships with people around you? Can you stay broken and can you stay humble? And can you bow when you see somebody higher than yourself, even though you may not agree with everything that they say? Can you embrace someone else, even though they may not be of the same beliefs all the way around with you?"

Enhanced social ministries

A hallmark of Rock City Church is its social outreach, from before the revival began to the time of this writing. Social programs make up the "Martha ministries" counterbalance to the "Mary ministries" of worship (Luke 10:38-42).

Social programs include

- "A Can Can Make a Difference," which annually provides many tons of free food to individuals and church food pantries in the Baltimore area
- "Adopt-a-Block," a program started by Rock City Church that works with other churches, social agencies, and the city of Baltimore to clean up and reclaim drug-infested inner-city blocks through placing church members as residents in houses or apart-

ments within those blocks
- "The Hiding Place," a shelter for women and girls, especially those in crisis pregnancies
- "Nehemiah's House," a shelter and rehabilitation center for homeless men

These programs, all of which were in place before the revival began, are funded almost exclusively by grants from various foundations. The church employs a full-time grant writer for that purpose.

All of the social programs took, in Pierce's words, "a remarkable turn up" when the revival began. He estimated that the tonnage of free food distributed to the needy through the church's "A Can Can Make a Difference" program increased 30 percent. In addition, the ministry was given new tractor-trailer trucks for delivering the food. Other new items, such as building supplies, also began to be donated. During the revival, the Nehemiah's House men's shelter added twenty-five new beds to the existing thirty-one. The Adopt-a-Block program continued to reclaim four to six inner-city blocks each year, and several homes were donated to the ministry.

A more direct spiritual influence was felt in the social ministries as well. K. C. Carter heads up some of these programs. He commented, "Adopt-a-Block was active before the revival began. We take back drug-infested blocks in the inner city. Since the revival started, the presence of God comes in there, right in the inner city, and we're seeing people getting saved. Not only that, we see pastors begin to work together right there in the inner city. Pastors call me and say, 'Man, I went to a block party [the first step in reclaiming a block]. Now I want to do that.' We're beginning to not just pastor our churches but we're beginning to pastor our cities."

One staff member related the enthusiasm this created in the church: "It was a Thursday afternoon, I looked in the newspaper, we had an article there. The first thought was, we are affecting the city."

It was not only organized social programs that were strengthened by the revival. Layperson Glenda Wooden told me of her own private social ministry movement: "My daughter and I go and knock on our neighbor's doors and just say, 'Hi!' We've frightened a lot of people, but it's amazing, I've had people come to me and say, 'We need food,' and we say, 'How can we help?' God has changed our hearts enough to know that every single person has a need. All of the kids come and during the summertime we would be handing lemonade out of the window. My sixty-five year old Jewish neighbor comes to me when he needs me to bandage his wound. I know he came to me because of what I've given him. The aging family that lives down the hall, they come to me. The young lady who lives around the corner, when she needed food, she came to me. Other kids, when they need to go places, they come ask me. And that's not because of who I am, because who I was, nobody came near me. You couldn't even walk across my path!"

This personal involvement didn't come about by accident. According to Kay Culver, Pierce taught his congregation, "Open your home, if you're in a position to do that. Have people over. Feed them, house and clothe them, help to meet their needs. Don't just think that something supernatural is going to fall on them. Be a conduit. Throw that fifty in that man's hand. Give those extra clothes to someone."

Culver commented, "We help in the natural, as well as with the spiritual needs, and I think that's what helps to keep the balance. Mary and Martha."

Rock City Church 24 Years Later

On March 17, 2023, twenty-four years after the study cited above, I spoke with Bart Pierce, now a Bishop, who recently celebrated his fortieth year as senior pastor of Rock City Church. Below is a transcript of that conversation, conducted by telephone from Missouri, slightly edited for relevance and clarity.

Bishop Pierce We were so blessed to be in that setting. We all got something to help us. All got something different, probably, but we all got something collectively that we knew God was in that house.

David Oh, no question. So what has God been doing there in the last 24 years?

Bishop Pierce Well, number one, I'm getting old. And that's okay.

David You didn't look it when I saw you online the other day.

Bishop Pierce Well I manage to dress up pretty nice.

What happened, David, is we went through the process of walking away from that. But it was not a quick turnaround for the process because we had re-ordered our whole life. We had re-ordered the church schedules, our personal life. We pulled one of my sons, my youngest son, out of school and homeschooled him. So we were in a process of at least a year of just kind of getting our feet back again into some form of normalcy, realizing we would never be the same again.

And that brought us into a place of, "Now what, Lord?" And God's presence, even to this day, if we are in a moment of prayer or moment of worship or something, and we really turn our faces towards him, it's not but a moment or two before his presence just rolls in.

We've always said, "Where he's been, he'll come again," and "God is attracted to his own presence."

We went and saw a gentleman named Edward Miller. He was used by God to start the Argentine revival with Tommy Hicks. And we went and met with him, Tommy [Tenney] and his wife and myself and my

CASE STUDY 1: ROCK CITY CHURCH OF BALTIMORE

wife. He was able to help us understand some things.

Tommy asked him, would the revival last? And Dr. Miller, without any hesitation, said no. He said they're not meant to last. They are to revive. It's like a dead person that gets the paddles put on their heart. They are revived and you don't keep shocking them. So we heard that. And my wife jumped in and she said, "Well, what do we do?" And he said, "You dig a well." You dig a well so that all that God did during those meetings and during those moments could flow into that well, and you would drink from that well the rest of your life.

That became our hope. That became something that we could really lay hold of, that those of us that had those moments in the presence of God, we would be able to go back to them at a moment's heart movement, and we could drink from that. And so that's really been a sustaining thing for many of us.

Of course, his presence is so strong still. We still make fresh bread for every service and we have it there on the altar [representing God's presence; see Exodus 25:30]. We don't always use it, but it's always there and people will take it at times and things happen.

We also play worship music 24 hours a day, seven days a week in the sanctuary, except when we're actually in there occupying it. We have on CD many of the music recordings that we produced and we have worship going on 24-7. That's kept the fire lit, sort of like Israel was told they had to keep the fire lit in the tabernacle constantly. So we've kept the fire going.

And the church has grown. We have a day school and it's just exploded. We have a camp for kids from June to August; this year, we'll have right about 500 kids at that camp. Our Bible school has tripled. In September we'll fully occupy an additional building. God's really, really just very graciously blessed us.

And we have over 130 churches now in other countries and around the nation. So God's multiplied just about every area that we could be involved in.

Right now, we feed about 65-68,000 people a month.

David My goodness, right there in Baltimore?

Bishop Pierce Right in Baltimore. Our warehouse is constantly moving food in and moving food out. Tractor trailers are constantly interacting with people up there. And so that's been a real big thing that's going on.

And then at the same time, we have a home for young women who get pregnant, and we've now had a little over 1400 babies born there.

So all of that just from those meetings. Some of it is new and some of it's just erupting in growth and blessings.

The other area that you might know is that we had a thing happening with pastors in the area called Peace for the City.

David I was part of that.

Bishop Pierce Okay. Well, we laid that aside a few years after we stopped the meetings. We had meetings for about four or five years, then we stopped those meetings. Now, relationships didn't stop, but the focused, concentrated meetings that we were having with those pastors, we laid that aside to see what God would say to do. And just the end of last year we got a real strong word to call the pastors back together again.

We've been doing that monthly now for the last probably seven months now, eight months, and April the ninth, which is Easter Resurrection Sunday, down in the harbor in Baltimore, we're having a sunrise service. And we have churches, I don't even know the number exactly right now, but we have over thirty-six bishops working with us from all around the area. It's a two-hour service. It starts at 6:30 in the morning, which, that'll be a miracle in itself.

David Praise the Lord.

Bishop Pierce It's about prayer. We're coming back together to pray and to just really ask God to heal this city and heal this area.

So that's kind of a short synopsis of what happened in the meantime. There are so many wonderful miracles and things that have happened in people's lives.

Tommy Tenney preached here about seven or eight months ago for the first time since he stopped coming to those meetings.

David I bet that was powerful.

Bishop Pierce Oh, it was very, very, very powerful. Tommy and I have been in communication but this was the first time he actually came back and preached. He's been traveling all over the world. And it was really good.

Folks like yourself or others who came in from other countries [for the revival meetings] will stop in. I ran into a guy in the Walmart about a week ago. I didn't see him. He saw me, came over, introduced himself, and he said, "Twenty-three years ago, you changed my wife's and my life. We'd been missionaries in Australia. We came to those meetings, you met with us and said come by tomorrow and see me," and for no reason that I would have known, he said I asked him, "Are you able to pay your current mortgage?" And he said, "No." And I went and got a check and I paid his mortgage. And he just told me, "It changed our whole life being in those meetings." And then he told me about what was happening in Australia, and he said a guy showed up to preach in Australia and they're in the outback. The guy came and they got talking, "Where are you from?" And the guy said, "Well, I'm originally from Baltimore." And the guy said, "Hey, did you ever go to this church called Rock City Church?" He said, "Well, yeah, yeah, I went there 23, 24 years ago," or whatever. But he said, "I went there, and I was searching for God and God changed my life and today I'm in full-time ministry."

We find people now all over the world. People in Israel will tell us they still listen to our worship music.

David I do, too, sometimes.

So that's the fruits of the revival carrying on.

Bishop Pierce That's right.

David Back to Peace for the City for a minute, are you still using the Baltimore Covenant?

Bishop Pierce Yes. What we did was we took it and added two more sections that included the next generation. A lot of the guys that originally were part of it are still. Some of the others are no longer in ministry because of health issues, and some of the other pastors died. So these younger pastors have come in and we're kind of helping them embrace what we did, but not make that the model they have to follow. Just encouraging them that they can do this. So we've added a couple of things in that covenant that would include them.

David As I interviewed you twenty-four years ago you were in the midst of it, and I got some wonderful information about pastoring revival. Is there anything you would like to add, anything you've learned as you thought about it over the intervening decades? Is there anything you'd like to pass on along those lines?

Bishop Pierce Well, I think, David, one of the things that we have witnessed is that you have to realize, first of all, that it's a sovereign thing and you can't just arbitrarily try to duplicate it. And if you keep that in mind, then you won't frustrate yourself by trying to say everything we do has to look like that.

What came was a wonderful outpouring. Our lives will never be the same. Now we have to bear the fruit of that outpouring, and that might look a lot different.

We had people, of course, who were with us through that period because they just wanted God. He just moved here. Once that moved on and that heavy weight of that lifted, they found themselves going on in life to other journeys and places and so forth — which is fine, which is wonderful. And you have to be able to embrace that and not see that as a decline of something. It's just another page in the book.

The worst thing you can do is look at the after-effect and become critical, questioning, "Why did it go, why did it lift?" It's never meant to stay. It's meant to revive us. And it's the fruit of what we walk in from that point on, that should be evidence that we had that.

David How did you know it was time to end the meetings with Tommy?

Bishop Pierce Three and a half years into it, God spoke to me one morning while I was in prayer and said, "Are you willing to let my presence go into other churches in the city?" And he gave me the example of what David did with the Ark, when he took the ark and put it in Obed-edom's house. And then he went back and retrieved it, and brought it into the city. [See 2 Samuel 6.] And I said, "I don't understand it, but Lord, sure." And immediately I was aware that Peace for the City had been set up so we'd have relationships to be able to say to these other pastors, "We're closing the meeting down. But you are more than welcome to have these meetings and run with them." And so being able to allow that to happen in other places and not become judgmental or jealous or critical.

Like with Asbury, when that outpouring took place. They've had that before, I think, three times there. And now there's the movie "The Jesus Revolution." That movie is profound because it has to do with the Jesus movement, which I was a part of.

David Me too, at the tail end.

Bishop Pierce We were at Virginia Beach, and we saw thousands of hippies get saved. And that was a gift. But then we moved on from that. And it's good to see it in reflection. But where you are today may not be where you are a year from now. The Scripture says we move from glory to glory to glory. We are changed into his image.

So that's what I say to pastors. They go, "Well, how do we get the revival to happen in our church?" And I tell them, "I don't have a clue." All I know is we were hungry for God. We were humble enough so that God could come in and interrupt everything. And that hunger, that humility, joined up with our prayers to want him, not just an event. And maybe, maybe, that opened the heavens.

David When I talked to you twenty-four years ago, we talked about things that could cut a revival short. I remember you saying that you had your staff read the Charles Finney list [see Chapter 10], among other things. And you emphasized having to pastor the members of the church who did not immediately jump into the revival and who maybe never did. I found those very, very important. Is there anything else along those lines about pastoring the church in the midst of a revival that you would like to add?

Bishop Pierce When you've had an experience like that, it can be intimidating when you talk to some group and you tell them about all the wonderful things that God did, and yet they're not having that experience. So you have to measure that out so that you don't make something unattainable. You tell them that there's more of God, but not make it so "you didn't have that" or "you weren't there." That would create negativity. So what we've tried to do is encourage people and the younger generation that they can have their own outpouring, they can have their own Jesus revolution, and not say it has to look like the one we had. But it must have certain characteristics which would be: God, His word, hunger for prayer, hunger for souls, and a huge dose of humility.

David Would you say those are the hallmarks of a genuine revival?

Bishop Pierce Yeah, I do.
I don't call Asbury a revival — that's just words, terminology — I try not to refer to what happened in Baltimore or what happened in Toronto or Brownsville, I don't think they were revival by the typical language associated with a revival.

For me, revival that I read about in the 1700s, 1800s, the Great Awakening, all those things with Charles Finney, all of those guys, Jonathan Edwards and all those guys, it changed nations. Whole nations were turned upside down. Inventions and creations came to the surface. Things happened that never could seemingly happen before.

So when I say "revival," it has to shake more than a university or more than a local church.

I mean, they tell stories when Azusa Street with Daddy Seymour broke out in 1906, the revival with Evan Roberts in Wales. 125,000 people got swept into the kingdom within a week. And Azusa Street, they were in the streets of San Bernardino, California, and L.A. and at night they would hear the songs sung out in the streets. Hundreds of hundreds of thousands of people were on fire for God. And when Charles Finney walked into factories up in New York, the factory people ceased to be able to work. They were on their faces weeping. And whole legislative bodies in Colorado shut down and out in Oregon they shut down the local legislative bodies and held prayer meetings every day at noon. Policemen formed choirs. Courts were shut down because there was no crime.

When you see what revival does, revival shapes nations. And so I just kind of stay away from saying this little outpouring — and I don't mean little by any measure, what happened with us will change our lives forever. But it was not a revival. It was an awakening, it was an outpouring, it was a visitation of God, only to make us hungry for a real revival.

David Amen. And I agree with you on the terminology. I just want to mention to you that I am using the term revival in my book just because that's what most people recognize.

Bishop Pierce Exactly. You're a hundred percent right. And that's why I qualified what I said. It's terminology, just words.

What I'm trying to say to you, as someone who's mature enough to understand this and was in those experiences enough that it's moved your heart to write about it, is that we must not ever be satisfied with something that's less than something that's greater.

David Thank you so much. You've answered the questions I had, and I really do appreciate your time.

5

Case Study 2: The Crossing

Washington Crossing United Methodist Church, informally known as "The Crossing," occupies a large, modern brick facility on a country road in affluent Bucks County, Pennsylvania, about forty miles north of Philadelphia and not far from Princeton, New Jersey. Originally housed in a historic church near the site where George Washington and his troops made their famous Christmas Eve crossing of the Delaware River, the congregation moved to its present building in 1985. It became the second case study for my dissertation at the urging of my advisor, Dr. Steve Seamands, who felt it was important to include an example of a mainline denominational church in revival.

Beginnings

Dr. Scott McDermott came to The Crossing in 1993. The previous pastor, who had served a long pastorate and built the new building, withdrew from the denomination to plant a new church a short distance away. About half of the seven hundred members went with him. Faced with a substantial mortgage and severe financial problems, McDermott modeled prayer and sacrificial giving. A year later, revival struck.

McDermott had not been teaching on or expecting a powerful move of God in his church. It began with a sermon on Nehemiah's seven days of rejoicing, which led to a week of "rejoicing services." On the second night, as people came forward for prayer, they began to fall to the ground under the power of the Holy Spirit. This was the beginning.

Despite publicity in the October 1998 issue of *Charisma* magazine, the revival drew few visitors.

Like Bart Pierce and Tommy Tenney, Scott McDermott was very helpful in facilitating my research. He told me via email that what he called "the work of renewal" in the church began in 1994. "From that time a work of transformation has begun."

Rev. McDermott believed what was happening at Washington Crossing was "at least a two-pronged effort." Along with the spontaneous move of the Spirit in renewal, specific pastoral leadership actions "such as the development of mission, vision, and philosophy of ministry statements, as well as the development of leadership issues within the staff and lay leadership" all contributed to the overall transformation of the church.

A Visit to The Crossing

Five years into the revival, the congregation was largely made up of young to middle-aged adults and their children. The two identical Sunday morning worship services featured a casual atmosphere and a contemporary praise band. Evening renewal and prayer services were attended almost exclusively by church members.

I visited Washington Crossing on May 15-16, 1999, arriving Saturday evening in time for the weekly renewal service. Dressed in coat and tie, I immediately stood out as a visitor among the casually attired parishioners, but I was warmly welcomed.

CASE STUDY 2: THE CROSSING

The sanctuary was furnished with padded stacking chairs, with ample open space at the front and rear. A band led perhaps eighty people in praise and worship, followed by a sermon by blue-jeaned assistant pastor Mike Sullivan, as Rev. McDermott was away.

The sermon ended with an altar call to which most of the people in the room responded, lining up in six or seven queues at the front of the sanctuary, where they patiently waited as teams of usually two people prayed for them. The prayers often took several minutes and almost invariably resulted in the person receiving prayer being slain in the Spirit.

Prayer is foundational at Washington Crossing. A recent addition to the services was a midweek time of "soaking prayer," where people were invited to bring pillows and relax on the floor in an atmosphere of quiet, receptive prayer for the evening.

Sunday morning, by invitation, I attended the 8:30 a.m. prayer meeting of the ministerial staff and musicians. There I met Rev. McDermott. A casual atmosphere again prevailed as jeans or khakis and polo shirts, or similar styles for the women, seemed the order of the day. Prayer was in a circle, not orchestrated but orderly. Occasionally someone would suddenly bend sharply at the waist and shout, "Oh!," an action common to those whose revival pedigree traces back to the Toronto outpouring.

At 9:00 a.m. the first service began, followed by an identical service at 11:00. Sunday services were held in the gymnasium using stacking chairs, the sanctuary having been outgrown. Attendance at each service was approximately four hundred people. The congregation was predominantly white, reflective of the demographics of the area. McDermott estimated the average age at twenty-nine. The casual dress reflected an intentional effort to make people of all socio-economic levels feel welcome.

The service began with praise and worship, followed by announcements, both live and via Powerpoint and video projection. The sermon was given by guest speaker Terry Teykl, author of a number of books on prayer. Rev. McDermott, in khakis and polo shirt, sat in the front row of the congregation. At the second service, he was joined there by his United Methodist District Superintendent, whose black suit stood out starkly in the comfortably dressed crowd. The two services were essentially identical, even though McDermott said he did not plan out the services beyond a simple formula of worship, sharing, and preaching.

Sunday evening I attended the weekly "Concert of Prayer." Approximately two hundred people met in the sanctuary for a time of praise singing and corporate prayer. After thirty to forty-five minutes they broke up into smaller groups which gathered around eighteen signs distributed around the room. The signs bore such inscriptions as, "Confession and Repentance," "Prayer for Revival," "Prayer for the Inner City," "Upcoming Events," "Our Ministerial Staff," and "Pray as the Spirit Leads You."

The prayer service ended with approximately twenty elementary-age children, who had just returned from a retreat, being invited to form two parallel lines facing each other. The adults then walked very slowly between the lines while each child laid hands on them and prayed. The adults were obviously affected by this "fire tunnel," most of them crying their way to the altar rail where other adults prayed with them.

I talked with senior pastor McDermott, assistant pastor Sullivan, and their wives over lunch that afternoon. The Sunday evening service afforded opportunity to speak with several laypeople, including key leaders. It is significant that most of the top lay leaders were among the 25 percent of morning attendance who came back for the evening meeting.

Characteristics

Seven characteristics defined the move of God at Washington Crossing.

1. The centrality of prayer
2. People being slain in the Spirit
3. Revival confined primarily to the local church
4. A casual atmosphere
5. Increased social action
6. An ongoing connection to the revival at Toronto Airport Christian Fellowship
7. Periodic waves of renewal

Prayer

The main defining characteristic of the revival at The Crossing was prayer. Randall Baker, chair of the church council and a veteran of leadership in a number of churches, told me, "The emphasis on prayer here is unbelievable." Church leaders intentionally underscored that emphasis when they moved the church library out of a prime location near the sanctuary and turned that space into a prayer room.

Scott McDermott remembered, "The night revival hit, I was praying for people." And when a new wave of revival came through in March of 1999, he said, "We got to the point of the teaching of the Word and I said, 'I'm not going to preach today. I'm just going to stay right here and pray and praise the Lord until I physically can't.'"

The congregation responded in kind. McDermott described the people's response that March Sunday morning. "We had people lining up. I came back that night for a prayer meeting, and I was really awed. We prayed in intercessory prayer for about two hours, then we prayed for individual people for three hours."

McDermott said God also invaded the staff prayer meetings. "I mean, hours of intercession. We couldn't even talk! The presence of God is so overwhelming. You have a striving very deep in you, deep private personal intercession. A couple of hours a day we've interceded. I felt called to keep praying more. I would pray about two hours a day. And then God just seemed to show up. What God wants, I think, is a feeling from the heart. And that can happen through prayer. You've got to pray."

It is easy to overlook the fact that McDermott was already holding regularly scheduled and well-attended prayer meetings for the staff, over and above the congregational prayer meetings, before the Lord "invaded" them.

Baker recalled, "We used to have a Sunday evening service with thirty to fifty people. Scott had this vision, or felt led, that Sunday nights, instead of having teaching or preaching, we'd be having a concert of prayer. We've been doing this two years or more, and it's two hundred people praying. You pray for something and God answers it. We try to lay down our agendas and see what God would want. We pray for it. Pray for unity, for revival."

Slain in the Spirit

In keeping with many other occurrences of the River revival, a clear characteristic of the movement at Washington Crossing was people being slain in the Spirit. McDermott remembered it being so from the start: "The night revival hit, I was praying for people, and they began falling on the floor. Our worship leader, Walter, he's an ordained Methodist pastor, goes down, and as he's going down, he said, 'I don't do this.' Well he did, and the room was aghast. And the next night we had over a hundred and twenty-five people—people dancing, about ten o'clock at night, people all over the floor."

The phrase, "people all over the floor," recurred several times in the interviews. It speaks to the prevalence of the phenomenon, not just in the initial outpouring, but as the revival continued.

Revival confined primarily to the local church

In contrast to the revival at Rock City Church, what happened at The Crossing seemed to be much more of a local church renewal. I was told it was rare for people from other churches to attend the renewal or revival services. God's focus at The Crossing seemed to have been on helping the Christians there attain a new relationship with God.

McDermott said, "What's remarkable is the life-changing, wonderful longing after God. People are sitting in our services, burning in their heart. Folks are getting saved at our regular Sunday services."

Layman Todd Phillips amplified. "People's value systems have changed. We're seeing the things of the world stripped off of them. We're seeing them equipped to serve the Lord."

A casual atmosphere

Another characteristic of the Washington Crossing revival was its casual atmosphere. The intentional informal dress has already been described. This attitude carried over into the worship. It was not at all casual in the sense of being irreverent. Instead, there was a casualness, a tolerance, about letting each person worship in his or her own way. At any one time, some people would be kneeling, others dancing, others quietly sitting with head bowed or with hands and face raised, while others could be lying prostrate on the floor.

Phillips compared the attitude to the classic charismatic church he came from. "What God has been doing here has been very charismatic. It has not been the emphasis on the gifts of the Spirit or the exercise of the gifts, but on the presence of God, and his passion for us, and his sovereign power to move and do things that would defy the typical charismatic boxes of how various moves of the Spirit work. It has been very different from that stand."

Increased social action

The Washington Crossing revival supported the idea that true revival will always result in social action. McDermott said one hundred people, one-seventh of his congregation at the time, regularly drove forty-five minutes to be involved in inner-city ministry in Philadelphia and in Camden, New Jersey. "We have one group of people that are going to Philadelphia prayer-walking through crackhouses and things like that. It's just amazing."

McDermott described a new partnership between the church school and an inner-city elementary school, with the children visiting each other's locations to develop relationships. He mentioned mission trips to Siberia, Africa, Azerbaijan, and Mexico, among other projects. These trips are "not missions-programmed. They're God touching people's hearts to go do these things."

Connection to the Toronto Revival

The Washington Crossing revival maintained an ongoing connection with the revival at the Toronto Airport Christian Fellowship. McDermott and members of his staff and congregation made regular visits, and McDermott was invited to speak there. He even took his District Superintendent to Toronto, with the result that local United Methodist pastors could earn continuing education units for making the visit.

CASE STUDY 2: THE CROSSING

Waves of renewal

At the time of the case study, God's move at The Crossing had been going on for over five years. During that time, there were a series of renewals or strengthenings of the move. In my 1999 interview, McDermott said, "It has been waves. Came a wave in '94, then God would blast certain spots of the church just unexpectedly: the men's retreat, women's retreat, youth retreat. People getting saved, shaking, just shaking in the power of God."

The Crossing 24 Years Later

On March 27, 2023 I spoke with Scott McDermott by telephone. He was still Senior Pastor at The Crossing, completing a long tenure which is a rarity in Methodism, where bishops normally appoint pastors to different churches every few years. Below is a transcript of that conversation, edited for relevance and clarity.

David What has God been doing with you and with The Crossing since I talked to you twenty-four years ago?

Rev. McDermott Well, it's been an interesting time as things have really evolved. I think the work kept getting deeper over the years. Our prayer ministry really expanded into other areas from since you were there. We now have healing rooms. We have prophecy rooms. We have inner-healing rooms. It's really been pretty incredible. And a number of my staff have gone on to start ministries and they're ministering around the world, which is really awesome.

I'm about to retire here in the next couple of months. I'm back in with Randy Clark. I just did seven lectures in the Holy Spirit at the graduate school so I'll shift to that part-time.

What's astounded me is how God's given us favor with the Methodist church. I cannot, for the life of me, believe that. I just can't believe it. I have had such favor from every bishop to renewal. I've seen openness to what we're doing. I've seen a willingness to receive what we were doing. It just challenges my paradigm. And people in the Conference [United Methodist regional body] have experienced some really interesting things, and they've made note of it. And I'm very thankful for that.

Life is full of ups and downs. I'm pastoring thirty years now in July. You go through many iterations. And you learn about the organization and renewal and how you get this thing to work together. And all kinds of things that just go with pastoring a church. It's really been a very interesting journey. God's been good. I mean, I can really say it's been really, really, really rewarding.

Doors opened up. I was teaching at SMU for ten years in their Doctor of Ministry program. And again, I found such openness to my journey. It was just unbelievable sharing about this vision encounter I had. It's been fascinating. It's been quite a journey.

David At the time, I was interviewing you because the church was considered actively in revival, part of the River. Would you consider that it still is? Or if not, how did it end?

Rev. McDermott It is, it is. It continued pretty intense for a while — I mean, it really still is — but, how do I describe it? It's still a renewal church, without a doubt. His presence comes.

I watched fires come and go around the country. A church would get lit up for a while and then sort of go away. And I thought, what is the difference? And one thing that I believe — now I have no documentation on this, it's totally anecdotal— is the commitment to intercessory prayer.

CASE STUDY 2: THE CROSSING

We had a weekly prayer meeting that went on for ten or fifteen years that had over a couple hundred people in it where you pray for a couple of hours. I mean, we're talking about some incredible meetings. And I really feel that revival is best supported with — you need the Word, obviously we can't discount the Scriptures — but the heart of revival is fueled by intercessory prayer.

It seems that God honors humility, right? God goes where he's wanted the most to be. And I think that is what prayer does.

I think people want an experience, but they don't understand that it's all through prayer. That's what deepens and sustains, you know? And I believe that was what allowed us to stay in this place longer than many did.

I mean the whole church changed, and it's still that way. Prophecy rooms, everything. It just all flows out of that.

I think there's a dimension of the prayer life of the pastor, which I think is very significant. And I think there's also a commitment to corporate intercession that makes a difference.

You know, in most churches the prayer meeting, it's like four or five people, and that's about it. We're talking about people who are hungry to intercede.

I think this heart for it is so key. The longest service we had was eight hours. I finished praying for the last person at 4:30 in the afternoon. Then they came back two hours later for three more hours.

I think the problem is, we want the thrills and chills and good feeling, but God's not after that. God's after our lives. And I believe the kingdom advances on intercessory prayer.

Now, here's what I wrestle with: the question was, you know, are we earning it? Is it like, required to pray?

I've talked to pastors about my prayer life. And they would just feel guilty because they go, "I'm not praying enough, I'm not—." You know, I get it.

I came to this conclusion. It's not well thought out but here's my feeling: prayer is not the means by which we *earn* the favor of God, it's the means by which we *receive* the favor of God. So when you're face down before him, that just deepens things. And I think in our situation, we're in a very affluent, highly educated area, I think God wanted us to know it's all about him and not about us. When you're in that place of humility, that's where God really works.

So we did it. Everything was formed in prayer. At our staff prayer meeting we prayed for an hour. Everything was based on prayer. And I think that people saw that. I mean, it really was.

If you really believe Wesley, who says God does nothing save in answer to prayer, how does that change what you do? It changes everything.

One night I had a friend coming from Georgia — I moved up here from Georgia — and he came into this prayer meeting on Sunday night. It was over 100, 200 people every week. So he's in this service. It just flows. There's worship happening, there's communion, people kneeling at the altar, there's prayers going. It's just free-flowing. I can't even describe, different every week. I said to him at the end, "How do you feel, tell me about your experience?"

He said, "I felt like I was in God's living room."

And I thought, that's it, you know?

And so, when you're in that place — I can have pastors come from the Conference, David, progressive pastors, you never could predict it. And I'll watch them, and they've come to me and said, "I love what you're doing." People can be so real before God. I love this.

Anyway, you get the idea. But I think prayer is the key element to it. I think that's the big lesson.

I'm concerned that people just want a good week of meetings or a few good moments. We need that, our hearts have to be reset. But if revival is not helping us to walk better you know something's missing.

CASE STUDY 2: THE CROSSING

It's just an emotional experience. Now we need to go deeper than that. That's what I think.

David I agree 100%. But let me ask you, I've experienced what you pointed out, that in most churches the intercessory prayer meetings are three or four people. I had the blessing to attend one of your Sunday evening intercessory prayer times and yes, hundreds of people there. Did that just happen, or is there something you did to create that hunger for prayer? As a pastor, how did you cause it, create it, feed it, or at least not get in the way of it?

Rev. McDermott Well, let me tell you, a funny thing happened. This lady really helped me out.

I had a really good prayer life. I prayed two hours a day. That was my regular intercession before revival broke out. I remember I couldn't even talk in the presence. I'd get here early and pray, and I couldn't even move, the presence of God was so deep on my life. And I didn't know what was happening.

I loved to pray, always prayed and would wait hours as a teenager when I came to Christ, but it was never like this. It was really very, very deep.

So I felt good when I was talking to this person that I was in a good prayer space. And she said to me, "Well, who are you praying with?"

I mean I had a pretty good prayer life, I could check off the list. But she said, "You need to pray with other people, you need to have a corporate prayer session." And it just stuck with me.

I based the style of the prayer meeting off my own personal prayer life. We had a Sunday night service and I said, "Let's make it a prayer meeting." I had no idea who would come, and I can't even tell you how many came the first time. I don't even remember how it grew. It just began to grow and people would just show up. It was just fun to watch

God work.

It's definitely a challenge to do that. There's something about seeking God together, right? But she's the one who challenged me.

David You say that you feel like you're still in revival. Is there a place where a church is done being in revival and becomes a revived church?

Rev. McDermott That's a good question. I think you need revival even though you're in revival. I think it's going to take an incremental physical revival. Don't go after revival, go after God's presence.

I think it's a title, you know? I know there are all these studies about what revival does. Are we still in it? How do you measure that? I think we always want more. I mean, look, we have incredible — people sense the presence of God when they walk into the building.

I have people from the Conference who are not evangelicals walk into the building and they go, "I really sense God's presence in here." I mean, we're talking about that kind of stuff.

Look, we want more, I'm sure we're not where we need to be. It can't be just, we sit around in a meeting because we're there.

The New Testament church, were they ever not in revival? The Book of Acts is thirty years of church history and the Spirit is being still poured out like twenty-something years after Pentecost. It happens to me. There's a measure of living in the Spirit, it's like we learn that this is how we live. I learned early on. God called. I felt the Holy Spirit. This is very humbling.

But God told me what was happening among us wasn't an experience to have. It was a lifestyle. It's not just a one-off "I had this happen to me." It's an invitation to an open door for a way of living.

It's not just about encountering the Spirit. It's about learning to walk in the Spirit. And I think that's where we are. Sure we'd like more encounters. This is part of who we are, but we want more. You still want revival.

Now are we in revival? That's a great question. I would say it depends how you define revival, right? What does that mean? I think it's about learning how to walk in the Spirit and grow in the Spirit.

But the things that God deposited are still there. And I think that it's really pretty awesome. I'm thankful for that.

David Absolutely. Is there anything else that you would like to add? My thought in particular was not so much the pastors who are really seeking and praying, but the pastors who have a layperson go to someplace like your church or like Asbury to visit and bring it back, and all of a sudden this stuff is happening in the congregation and the pastor kind of is blindsided and they start looking for books on what do I do now? Do you have any advice for that kind of a situation?

Rev. McDermott I think pastors take congregations across thresholds.

When God visited The Crossing, the weird thing was it just happened. We didn't seek it. I didn't teach on it. I didn't teach on the Holy Spirit. I'd been there a year. What was about to happen none of us saw coming. It just happened.

So I was going down to Brownsville and teaching a seminar for pastors, and I realized that our model isn't typical. The typical model is this: it's tell and show. You can teach them and then they can experience it. That is typical. That's the best way to lead. Help you understand.

But there are times when God has to show and tell. It's the opposite. It's like the day of Pentecost. He just shows up. And then you have to explain that, like Peter did. People are going, "What's happening?"

It's much easier to criticize than it is to lead. You can stand in a revival movement in the congregation and critique the guy on the platform until it's happening in front of you and you go, "Wait a minute, what's going on here?" It's a different ballgame. And you're trying to really discern the Spirit in those moments. You've got to work through it.

Here's my takeaway: when these waves of the Spirit come, ride the wave as far as it will take you. Practically speaking, you can't do it forever. I mean, Toronto did it for years, but they couldn't find their church after the first few months. Who's here and who's not?

And Asbury had to go back to normal life. They couldn't quite keep going. So there's elements of practical sustainability. That's really true. And you have to look at it. But when these waves come — we had several waves come, more than several — you ride them. It's hard to see. You're aware that all of the sudden this is just not happening anymore. But you take that for as long as you can take it and you sort of just go with it and see what you learned. In those days of extended meetings you learn more in a week than you'd learn in ten, twenty years.

We had an outbreak happen in 2008, an amazing healing. It was unbelievable. We had a guy get out of the wheelchair and walk. He hadn't walked in two or three years. I mean, the air left the room. It was out of the box. I watched this guy every week come to church and this guy brought him in a wheelchair, wheeling him into the church. I mean, it was unbelievable.

So you have these moments come, and you lean into them. You learn from it and you watch how God moves and it's pretty astounding.

I still keep curious and keep learning, keep reflecting. And when the moment comes, step through the door. When God opens the door, just step through it.

And you don't try to make it happen. It's a hard thing. I mean what's hard is knowing that passive and active part. It's more of an art form than a science.

I know you have to pursue revival, but sometimes they just try to get the emotions all worked up. Actually, I think that's what made Asbury so beautiful. It's so pure. You want that purity in it. And that's what

I think makes it an art form. It's a sense of, I can't even describe it. But when the moment comes you jump through it, take it for what it's worth, and you learn from it and then you grow in it. And this is how God really changes our lives and really uses us.

I would rather go to church on a Sunday morning and not come out and say, how great was the pastor, the sermon was fantastic, or how great was the worship, it was fantastic. I want to come out of church and say, wasn't God amazing? And that's what's missing. It's about the superstar preacher, the superstar worship leader. And, you know, it's not. Church is about his presence.

When you travel in the world, you realize it's about his presence. That's what sustains the church. And I think revival reminds us, the Asbury revival, it's about him. It's not about us. It's not about our agenda. It's not about how big our church is, how big our budget is. It's about hearing his voice. It's about being willing to be used again. And God in revival presses the reset button. It's like everything goes back to "this is the priority." And you begin to live that, and that's what causes this advancement forward in the Spirit. And God begins to move. More than you know.

I mean, that's all it is. But, you know, different roles in the kingdom, how God uses us. I've been thankful that God's allowed me to see what I'm seeing in my lifetime.

6

Case Study 3: The Author's Experience

> *My message and my preaching were not with wise and persuasive words, but with a demonstration of the Spirit's power, so that your faith might not rest on human wisdom, but on God's power.* — 1 Corinthians 2:4–5 NIV

God has allowed me to experience revival from three different perspectives: seeker, pastor, and student. Beginning sometime in the 1990s, the above passage was the key verse that guided my life and ministry. (For the first ten or so years it was Joshua 1:8, and since I retired from pastoral ministry and began writing it has been 2 Timothy 2:2.) Experiencing, sharing, and understanding the Holy Spirit of God in all the ways he works and reveals himself has been my passion.

Mr. Wentz, Seeker of Revival

I was born and raised in a church-going family in Maryland. Growing up believing in God, I can't say for certain when I first crossed the line between being lost and being saved in terms of where I'll go when I die. But I can pinpoint when I gave myself completely to God. It was the summer of 1972, when I was eighteen, at a Young Life camp in Colorado.

On Wednesday evening of the week at camp, a speaker explained the gospel, then told us all to go spend twenty minutes alone with God and pray. I felt I truly wanted to commit my life to follow Jesus. At that time the most important thing in my life was my saxophone. I told God if he wanted me to dig a hole and bury my sax and never play it again, I would. It was the best way I could think of to illustrate how serious I was.

If it's more of God, I want it!

Later that summer I was invited to a Full Gospel Businessmen's meeting. It was 1972, and the Jesus Movement was spreading across the nation. I was one of perhaps five hundred people there. Indonesian evangelist Mel Tari gave a message on the baptism in the Holy Spirit. I didn't know what that was, but I thought, *If it's more of God, I want it.* This is not the place to debate various theological views of the Holy Spirit, his baptism, and his gifts. What I will say is that I received a prayer language that night that has been an important part of my life ever since.

"If it's more of God, I want it" pretty much sums up my attitude. I understand that God is one, in a fully orthodox Trinitarian way, and in that sense, I can't have more or less of God; I either have God in my life or I don't. I also understand that some would turn that around, and say the issue is letting God have more or less of me. Since that night in Colorado, I have done my best to let God have all of me.

It's been said that some Christians have more faith in the devil's ability to deceive us than in God's ability to keep us. My view has always been the opposite: I will seek God in any way that doesn't go against the Bible, and trust God not to let me get off track.

I know the dangers of false spiritual experiences. On the other hand, in Luke 24:25 Jesus said that being slow of heart to believe is foolishness. It's not an intellectual condition. It has nothing to do with intelligence or education. It's an attitude of the heart. Paul told us love believes all things (1 Corinthians 13:7). If something purports to glorify Jesus, I will give it every chance to do so.

The guiding principle is 1 Thessalonians 5:21–22 (ESV): *Test everything; hold fast what is good. Abstain from every form of evil.* Or as I heard a country preacher put it, "Be as smart as an old cow: swallow the grass and spit out the sticks."

Isaiah promises, *Your own ears will hear him. Right behind you a voice will say, "This is the way you should go," whether to the right or to the left* (Isaiah 30:21 NLT).

Almost exactly that happened to me a few weeks after that Full Gospel meeting, when I was invited to hear another speaker. During a break, I distinctly heard a voice saying, "There is a spirit of error here." I took the warning and never went back. It turned out to be a pseudo-Christian cult that could have led me into a morass of error.

That was the only time I ever heard God speak in what seemed like an audible voice. I believe he did it that time because he knew I was sincerely seeking him and I was in spiritual danger, and I was too much of a spiritual new-born to recognize his voice any other way.

Systematic theology!

That fall I began studies at the University of Virginia, with a major in systems engineering. One day I ran across a book about systematic theology. I was fascinated. Imagine capturing all knowledge about God through systems theory! I could see myself putting it all together, neatly explaining how God works in flow charts and diagrams.

CASE STUDY 3: THE AUTHOR'S EXPERIENCE

As I began trying to apply my scant knowledge of systems theory to the little I knew of theology, suddenly I was overwhelmed with a sense of the arrogance of my trying to define and codify God in that way. Ever since I have had a healthy terror of "boxing God in" and so limiting my ability both to recognize and join in his graceful, sovereign actions in my life and the world. Instead, I was reinforced in my desire to be open to new spiritual experiences, as long as they promise to glorify Jesus and are not clearly against the Bible. That attitude has guided the rest of my life.

God used my four years in college to begin widening my experience of Christian spirituality. I attended churches from Baptist to Catholic to Episcopal to a Jesus Movement commune. I played in what was then called a "Jesus rock band" and attended some of the first "Christian Woodstock" Jesus Festivals.

One evening in my third year in college, shortly after getting married, I felt God saying he would call me to some kind of ministry, but the time was not yet. So in 1976 I completed my degree, moved to Michigan to work as an engineer at Ford Motor Company, and became active in a small Church of the Nazarene congregation.

We were only in Michigan a little over two years, but it was there, in the context of that little blue-collar Nazarene church, that my greatest spiritual growth occurred.

I say "in the context" of that church, because the growth didn't come from a formal church activity. Rather, a group of seven or eight young adults from the church began meeting in each other's homes one night a week for Bible study. We didn't follow a program, and none of us had any theological education. The pastor was aware of our gathering but not involved. Yet the prayers, personal sharing, and informal collaborative Bible study in that small group resulted in more growth than any other experience of my life.

Jesus Revolution land

In 1978 I felt God leading me to leave my engineering career and enter seminary. After much prayer, consultation, and investigation, Paula and I and six-week-old Joshua packed up and moved to Santa Ana, California, where I enrolled at Melodyland School of Theology. The name came from the Melodyland Theater, which had been donated for use as a Bible school with the proviso that the name be retained. It was right across the street from Disneyland, and during breaks in evening classes, we could see the fireworks going up over Snow White's Castle.

Melodyland was not fully accredited, but it was one of only two seminaries I could find that were teaching about the baptism and gifts of the Holy Spirit. The other was the Assembly of God Graduate School, which had a prerequisite of New Testament Greek. Greek had not been part of my engineering curriculum, and I recognized some of the Melodyland professors as authors of books I'd read, so Melodyland it was.

I'm not sure I fully appreciated it at the time, but at Melodyland I was right at the source of the Jesus Revolution, both geographically and theologically. Chuck Smith's Calvary Chapel was twenty minutes away, where our landlord played bass on arguably the first contemporary praise and worship music record album, recorded there by Maranatha Music. Half an hour in the other direction, John Wimber was just beginning the Bible study that grew into the Vineyard Churches. And I remember a guest lecture at the seminary by one of Oral Roberts' healing revival colleagues, who gave us practical tips on how to recognize and follow God's lead in large meetings.

During this time I went to as many revival meetings as I could, though they weren't usually called that. It was at one of these that I was first slain in the Spirit.

For me, it was a very peaceful, non-emotional experience. At the end of the service, the speaker invited to the front anyone who wanted prayer. I forget the specific wording, but I took it as, "anyone who wants more of God." That was me! So I went up, along with scores of others. The preacher laid his hand on people's heads in turn and prayed for them. Some remained standing; others fell to the floor, eased down by "catchers" stationed behind them. When he gently touched my forehead, I remained conscious, not trying to fall but not trying to resist. I sagged back into the hands of the catcher and was lowered to the floor. For several minutes I lay there. There were no great revelations, but a wonderful sense of peace. Then I got up and returned to my seat.

Melodyland sought to cater to all denominations, but most students went on to pastor non-denominational churches. However, after much prayer and investigation, I felt God was leading me to the United Methodist Church, largely because they were open to my charismatic experience.

As I worked my way through the rather involved United Methodist pre-ordination path, I was repeatedly told, "You can do this step, but as long as you're at that unaccredited seminary, you can't do the next one." My reaction was always, "Well, I know God has called me to this, so that's God's problem." When my next meeting with the District Committee on Ordination rolled around, invariably something had changed, and I was allowed to continue to the following step.

A pastor but still seeking

Sure enough, after three years of full-time study, in 1981 I received my (unaccredited) Master of Divinity degree from Melodyland, and was appointed pastor of two small United Methodist congregations in Maryland. I was allowed to transfer two years of M. Div. credits to Wesley Theological Seminary, a United Methodist school in Washington, D.C., and studied part-time until I received my second M. Div. there. I used to joke that I should mount the charismatic and mainline diplomas back-to-back, and turn the appropriate one to face outward depending on who came into my office.

After the mandatory trial period, I became a fully ordained United Methodist pastor in 1988.

I continued to seek more of God. In the 1980s I attended church growth conferences featuring Paul Yonggi Cho, John Maxwell, and Robert H. Schuller, healing ministry conferences by John Wimber, and services by Kenneth Hagin and Benny Hinn. I also went several times to large inner-city African-American Pentecostal churches to hear speakers like Kenneth Copeland and Larry Lea.

My first experience in the River occurred when I heard South African evangelist Rodney Howard-Browne as he was just coming to prominence. Having first seen "holy laughter" and people "slain in the Spirit" on a small scale almost twenty years before, I was not taken aback by these phenomena.

In the next four years, my family and I visited the Toronto Airport Christian Fellowship, site of the longest-running continuous revival in North America. I experienced a number of the various streams that make up the River, including a Morningstar conference on prophetic ministry and revival meetings led by Rodney Howard-Brown and Randy Clark. I attended three of Rock City Church's "Peace for the City" retreats and the international "Light the Nations" conference featuring major leaders of revival from Argentina, Canada, the United States, and other nations.

CASE STUDY 3: THE AUTHOR'S EXPERIENCE

There's always more

In all these, I don't think I can remember a time when I did not respond to an invitation for prayer. One of Randy Clark's early books is titled *There's More*. My attitude continued to be, *If there's more of God, I want it*. And God is infinite, so there's always more.

As the twenty-first century dawned the River movement began to wane. I continued to seek out opportunities to attend services and conferences, but to be honest, many of them began to seem more and more like charismatic hype than genuine revival. Much of that, I'm sure, was well-intentioned preachers trying to hold on to God's presence by continuing to do what seemed to work before. Some, though, gave the appearance of purely human effort. Seeking God, for me, began to revolve more around small groups and my private devotions.

As I write this, I have retired from pastoral ministry and moved to a very rural area where big-name traveling preachers are not likely to come. But I continue to seek revival. Even before Asbury I saw things in small towns and country churches that I believe are the birth pangs of revival to come.

Rev. Wentz, Pastor of Revival

I served as a full-time United Methodist pastor from 1981 to 2015. During that time I pastored six congregations in five places in Maryland. (In the first appointment, like many beginning Methodist pastors, the bishop assigned me to serve two small churches at the same time). In 2015 I retired and moved to the Missouri Ozarks, where from 2016 to 2020 I pastored a small church part-time in retirement.

During those 38 years of pastoral ministry, I never stopped seeking to bring revival to the congregations I served. None of them experienced a sudden outpouring of the Holy Spirit like that seen in Toronto,

Brownsville, Smithton, Rock City Church, or The Crossing, but I believe they were revived nonetheless.

The fact is, most pastors will never have the kinds of experiences related in the previous two case studies. I just named five churches in which major outpourings of the Holy Spirit occurred as part of the River Movement. There may have been more, but those were all I can think of. At the same time, countless thousands of pastors attended services at those churches and sought to carry embers of revival back to their congregations. I was one of those thousands.

It would be great if God chooses your congregation as one to whom he will send a major outpouring of the Holy Spirit. Part of my motivation in writing this book is the hope that if more pastors and congregations are prepared to receive it, he will send it to them. However, if the next revival follows the pattern of past history, it will come to most churches as embers carried from another place. I include this section in hopes that you may learn something from my own efforts as a pastor in revival trying to carry it to the congregations I served.

Worship wars

When I began pastoral ministry in 1981 it was still common to hear a certain kind of pastor preach that "rock-and-roll is of the devil." It must have been something about the music they objected to because their opinion didn't change no matter how worshipful the lyrics. You might find the occasional acoustic guitar in country churches, but electric guitars and rock-and-roll backbeats were met with suspicion among pillars of the church almost everywhere.

I, on the other hand, was a product of the Jesus Revolution, coming from playing in a Jesus Rock band in college and three years of seminary in the birthplace of Contemporary Christian Music. I was still young enough that when I started in ministry, a grizzled old country blacksmith took one look at me and proclaimed, "They sent us a dad-blamed schoolboy!" For me, expressing Christ through rock-and-roll was only natural.

Despite what some of my older parishioners may have thought, I didn't introduce contemporary music to be rebellious. For me, praise and worship music with modern instruments was the soundtrack of revival.

I was moved from the two churches of my first appointment before I had a chance to do more than introduce the idea of modern music.

In my seven years at the next church, I began a contemporary service that eventually drew a larger attendance than the traditional one. This was the period between the Jesus Revolution and the River Movement. That church experienced some significant divine healings and other miracles, including a woman whose hearing was restored after being lost to nerve damage in a brain cancer operation, but none of these first churches experienced anything like the kind of revival we're talking about in this book.

Importing revival

In 1990 I was appointed to a church south of Baltimore whose history dates to before the American Revolution. Still meeting in the small white clapboard church erected in the 1880s, when I came they offered two identical services at 8:30 and 11:00 am.

A year or so after arriving, I started a contemporary service at 9:30, meeting in the church Fellowship Hall, which was in a separate education building. As at the previous church, this grew to be the largest service, though attendance at the traditional services remained stable. Discipleship, service, and outreach expanded, but again no sudden outpouring of revival. One couple thanked me for introducing them to more experiential worship, then left for the Assemblies of God where they could worship that way all the time!

It was during this time that I became aware of the River movement. I read all I could about it, took my family to Toronto to attend a revival service, and heard revival speakers whenever possible. When I learned what God was doing at Rock City church I attended as often as I could, often taking my family or church members. As a pastor, I longed to bring this move of God to the people under my care.

My approach was to preach on the relevant Biblical passages, mention my own experiences, and invite those interested to come back at a different time to hear more. This followed the pattern of revivalists of two hundred years ago, who preached the gospel in the morning and invited people to return in the evening for a seekers meeting.

In our case, what I invited people back to was a Sunday evening praise and worship service. I called it First Corinthians Fellowship, after Paul's summary of the New Testament's longest section on public worship in chapters 11-14 of 1 Corinthians:

> *Well, my brothers and sisters, let's summarize. When you meet together, one will sing, another will teach, another will tell some special revelation God has given, one will speak in tongues, and another will interpret what is said. But everything that is done must strengthen all of you.* (1 Corinthians 14:26 NLT)

When we began First Corinthians Fellowship in mid-1997 we met one Sunday evening a month. Soon those who were coming asked if we could we double that. The bi-monthly schedule continued for the next two and a half years.

The format was similar to that of evening revival services in other churches in the River, except that there was no formal preaching, and we did not receive an offering. First Corinthians Fellowship was a no-time-limit gathering for praise, worship, and whatever the Holy Spirit wanted to do. It never drew a large attendance, but it radically changed the lives of those who attended, and many others through them.

Most of those who came normally attended the contemporary service, which met in the Fellowship Hall. However, we chose to hold First Corinthians Fellowship in the church sanctuary, because it seemed like a more worshipful setting. As a pastoral issue, even that decision faced some blowback. Some dyed-in-the-wool traditionalist members had opposed starting the contemporary service because they didn't like "that kind of music," even though it was at a separate service in a different building. When they found that on Sunday nights guitars and drums were being played right in the sanctuary they were not happy. But by this time the contemporary service had been around for a couple of years, the sky had not fallen, and some of the new people attracted by the new music had turned out to be pretty good folks after all. When these things were gently pointed out, the rumblings died down pretty quickly. As pastor, I tried to smooth the way by reminding long-time members of what I called their long "tradition of innovation" in years past, including holding summer services in an outdoor Chapel in the Woods and parking lot "church in your car" services.

Our faithful praise band members began showing up around 5:30 pm. They had already set up and torn down the drum set, instruments, and sound equipment once that day in the Fellowship Hall. Now they did it all over again in the sanctuary.

The gathering began at 6:30. It would often not end until three hours later. As I look back I am amazed at the dedication of the band members, who may not get home until after 10:00 pm, with many going to work early the next morning. Yet they did this twice a month for two and a half years. Obviously, they felt God was doing something they thought made it worthwhile.

We began with music. I led the band and wrote many of the songs. Much of the other music was written at Rock City Church or was popular contemporary praise and worship. As time went by, several church members wrote songs, usually as poems which they asked me to set to music. Historically, most revivals have spawned their own music, as people open themselves to the creative gifts of the Holy Spirit.

We would start with a tentative playlist of perhaps twenty songs. As the evening wore on, I tried hard to be open to the Holy Spirit's guidance as to what songs to play, often skipping songs or rearranging the order. We usually began with a number of upbeat, joyful, even fun songs, expressing the joy of the Lord which was such a big part of many streams of the River, with everyone on their feet and many people dancing in the aisles. I gave no direction about this other than to encourage people to freely express their worship and not worry about what other people would think about them. I often told them, "I hate to break this to you, but they're not thinking about you at all!"

Gradually the songs would begin to express more intimate worship. When it seemed the time was right, usually after about an hour, we laid the instruments down, took a seat, and listened for a message from God.

This never involved a prepared sermon. Someone might share a prophetic word, usually starting not with the classic Pentecostal "Thus saith the Lord," but with the more charismatic or third-wave formulation, "I feel like God is saying . . ." These would be informally evaluated according to 1 Corinthians 14:29 NIV, *Two or three prophets should speak, and the others should weigh carefully what is said*. On rare occasions there might be tongues and interpretation, evaluated the same way.

Sometimes I would feel led to share something, never more than about five minutes, and rarely prepared in advance. Usually, I just

CASE STUDY 3: THE AUTHOR'S EXPERIENCE

opened it up for anyone who felt they had something to share. Most often this was a testimony of what God was showing someone or doing in their life. Several people might share in a given evening, speaking from their seats and often building on each other. As pastor, I tried to maintain a balance. I encouraged people to speak and thus gain confidence in their ability to hear from God and share what they were hearing. At the same time, I tried not to let it degenerate into a discussion of opinions or recounting of anecdotes, or let one person dominate.

Sharing time transitioned into ministry time, when members of the congregation gathered around and laid hands on those requesting prayer. Over the two and a half years the services were held, many later reported answered prayer of various types, several testified to immediate divine healings, and a handful of people were slain in the Spirit. It was not uncommon for people to report seeing angels in the sanctuary.

As pastor, I chose not to sensationalize any of this, or even publicize it outside the church. Those who experienced these phenomena were free to share with friends and other members of the congregation as they desired. Nonetheless, some leaders in the Baltimore River movement visited twice and encouraged me that what was happening in First Corinthians Fellowship was a small but valid stream of the River. As with Washington Crossing, our services attracted very few visitors. In our case, in addition to my lack of publicizing the services, this is probably because "revival tourists" visiting Maryland would have been attracted to the better-known services at Rock City Church.

First Corinthians Fellowship attracted a very loyal following, but never a very large one. At the time it was happening our average Sunday attendance was around 40 at the 8:15 traditional service, 70 or 80 at the 9:30 contemporary service, and 60 at the 11:00 traditional service. Attendance at First Corinthians Fellowship averaged 25-30. Almost all of them came from the contemporary service. Revival had certainly come to the church, but not all the church had come to revival.

In fact, this was not unusual. Even congregations that experience a massive outpouring of the Holy Spirit have their late adopters and holdouts. As a pastor, I had to be careful not to let my enthusiasm for what God was doing on Sunday evenings distract me from ministering to those who were not involved in it.

After about two and a half years, several of the most consistent attenders moved out of the area, including a key member of the band. Some other regulars became embroiled in strong disagreements over some church administrative issues. After prayer and discussion with the remaining attenders, it became clear that it was time to end the bi-monthly First Corinthians Fellowship gatherings.

Even though only a relatively small part of the church membership were active in these services, the flame of revival they represented had a profound effect on the church as a whole.

- Attendance at the two traditional services remained strong while the newly started contemporary service grew to become the largest of the three. At all three services the worship space was comfortably full, and the parking lot was stretched beyond capacity
- Giving increased, allowing many new ministries as well as hiring additional staff and air-conditioning the hundred-year-old church building
- Attendance at weekly Bible studies increased
- A deaf congregation that had shared the building for many years was taken into full partnership in a new Cooperative Parish, with the pastor of the deaf church also becoming a part-time associate pastor of the hearing church

A number of new ministries were begun, almost all of them initiated and overseen by lay volunteers active in the revival services. These included:

- Monthly Christian rock concerts featuring bands from the Baltimore/Washington area
- Monthy community breakfasts
- Mission trips
- Participation in the local Thanksgiving parade, with the praise band playing on a float
- An evangelistic outreach offering free bottles of water at a local flea market
- An adult literacy program
- A care and counseling ministry
- A youth band
- Monthly "Rest and Restoration" times in the sanctuary featuring an hour of live harp music to aid people in "soaking in the Holy Spirit"
- Even an evangelistic Christian mime troupe!

In addition, several laypeople active in First Corinthians Fellowship went on to ministries beyond the local church:

- Three women who had had abortions in the past began a regional ministry to help other women find not only God's forgiveness for their sense of guilt, but also healing from the spiritual and emotional trauma they experienced
- Michael Goins was instrumental in the growth of the international Transformation Project Prison Ministry
- Ray and Kathryn Leight founded Faith by Grace, a national ministry focused on helping people find inner healing and freedom in Christ

The church may have never experienced a sudden overwhelming outpouring of the Holy Spirit, but I think all these accomplishments from such a small group of people certainly testifies to his working in revival.

Reviving the remnants of a church split

In July of 2001, about six months after First Corinthians Fellowship ended, the bishop transferred me to another church. I followed a pastor who was retiring after over thirty years in that congregation, a very unusual length of time among Methodists. Under his leadership, the congregation had grown from twenty or thirty in attendance to over six hundred. For many members he was the only pastor they had ever known.

Theologically, the retiring pastor and I were very similar; in fact, I had considered him a mentor. Ecclesiologically, however, we were quite different. He had cultivated a vision for the congregation of becoming a pastor-centered mega-church. Indeed, three Sunday morning services averaging around 650 total attendance were filling the available space, and he already had an architect's drawing for a new building.

Shortly after I replaced him, church leaders asked me for my vision for the church. I didn't have a ready answer, but after some weeks of prayer, I told them what I felt God was showing me.

A strong and vibrant structure of small groups was in place involving perhaps 80% of the regular attenders. I proposed that instead of constructing an expensive new sanctuary, we have a rotating one-quarter of the small groups meet for church in homes each Sunday morning. This would open room for visitors in the services. In addition, my philosophy is that any two Christians should be equipped and motivated to be the church and have church any time, any place, with anybody (Matthew 18:20). This plan would automatically develop new lay leadership to do that.

I thought it was a great idea. But the response of the leaders was, essentially, "No, not that vision! Tell us the megachurch vision!"

The retired pastor and his family, contrary to denominational policy, had continued to be active in the church. When, after three years, it became clear that I was not going to adopt his megachurch vision, he and two staff members left and planted another church fifteen minutes away. Their first service was on Easter Sunday. They took with them over a third of the people, most of the lay leadership, and most of the main givers, and left behind a mortgage, a large missions commitment to support, and a very demoralized congregation.

I refused to call it a church split, though that was clearly what it was. Instead, I talked about two different plants growing in the same pot which needed to be separated into different pots so each could grow. As one of the staff members who had left was put forward as the pastor of the new church, I chose to see it, for myself and for the congregation, as him following God's call to step out by faith into a new ministry. I refused to let bitterness take root in myself or in those left behind. Instead, on the last Sunday before they left I called the staff member up to the front and prayed for him and the new church he was starting.

Then I prayed, preached, and worked for revival among those who remained.

As at the previous church, there was no great outpouring of the Holy Spirit over the whole congregation. Again, I was a pastor in revival trying to bring it to my church, carrying the fire and trying to create spiritual hunger in the people.

I had inherited a Sunday morning schedule of a small traditional service in the old sanctuary followed by two contemporary services in the gymnasium. Part of the contention with leaders who left was my refusal to cancel the traditional service. It had not been unusual in the contemporary services for people, especially youth, to come to the front to kneel and pray at the end of worship.

I put a rug in a corner of the gym at the foot of a large wooden cross, and invited people to make their way there to pray at any time during the service. It soon became common to see ten or twenty people kneeling there. Some were worshiping. Others were praying for God to move in the service and the church. Others, praying for a personal need, usually had someone else praying with them. After the service, I joined trained lay ministers in personal prayer for these requests.

In preaching for revival, I chose not to focus on external phenomena such as laughing, crying, or being slain in the Spirit. Instead, I encouraged openness to the Holy Spirit and whatever he wanted to do in each person's life, and taught about how to hear from God and respond with faith. I also introduced the concept of soaking in the Holy Spirit, and made opportunities for people to experience it. I consciously tried to raise expectations, otherwise known as faith, that each one could personally experience God's presence.

A week of prayer

The closest we came to a big outpouring of the Holy Spirit at this church was during a week of prayer in the summer of 2005. In some ways it was similar to an old-fashioned scheduled revival meeting. We had services nightly for six nights, and the objective was to revive faith and passion. However, the focus was not on preaching or evangelism, or even intercession or petition. Our requests centered on asking God to provide us with strategies, resources, and effectiveness in carrying out his call for us. But the real goal was for each person, not just the pastor or those in leadership, to hear from God and share the results.

Attendance each night averaged forty to fifty people. This was only about one-sixth of the post-split Sunday attendance, but it included most of the church leaders and a gratifying number of youth. Over the

CASE STUDY 3: THE AUTHOR'S EXPERIENCE

course of the week perhaps a third to half of the congregation came at least once.

After some musical praise and worship and a few words of instruction on the night's focus, I released everyone for about half an hour to visit different places in and around the church. They could visit prayer stations set up for different ministries and concerns in different parts of the building and property, walk a prayer labyrinth, or do whatever God led them to do. Throughout, they were encouraged to listen for what God might be telling or showing them. At the end, everyone gathered again for a time of sharing.

I urged people to write prayers on sticky notes. By the end of the week the wooden cross was covered with confessions, one wall was papered with thanksgivings and praise, and another wall with prayer requests.

All this was encouraging. But where I really saw the Holy Spirit moving was in people's openness to listening prayer, receiving and sharing what they felt God was saying or showing them. This was not limited to just the few members with a charismatic background. Many experienced this for the first time.

I asked everyone to write down what they felt they were receiving from God. Here is a small sample.

From a young woman:

> *I walked into the stairwell by the elevator and thought about how it is one of the least used spots in the church. I just had to stop and cry. And pray for the dark spots and hidden corners. I didn't get farther. I just sat and repeated that to God and cried.*
>
> *I also realized I was right by the door and I "should" move. But I couldn't. And later I realized why (after the weeping let up.) We are always in danger of someone opening the door to our dark spots and hurting us. We shouldn't have dark spots - no cobwebs,*

no dust, no places we don't go. God wants His lights there.

The prayer is corporate and for individuals. And it's from God. I wasn't seeking it — I was utterly surprised by bursting into tears in the stairwell.

Our darkness needs to come to light.

From a member of the church council, an engineer not normally given to this kind of thing:

My prayer: Lord, may we (the [church] family) be conscious of your spiritual kingdom and aware of your provisions.

The Lord's Response:

- *A Vision: I saw a man who looked like Jesus, that is he looked like the more common portraits and portrayals of our Lord. He was looking up while he was standing outside in the middle of a thunderstorm. With his hands outstretched to the rain coming down on him, he was smiling. I interpret the storm to be our challenges and the rain to be God's provision.*
- *A Word: [The church] is a tool for God's use. I interpret this to mean we are to be useable.*
- *A Word: [The church] is to reflect God's glory. I interpret this to show us how he will draw people to [the church]; and, once again, we must be able to reflect — we must be holy (1 Peter 1:15-16).*
- *A word: This time is not about the survival of "our" church. I interpret this to mean that no one should forget whose church this is...it belongs to God.*

My request: That you [leaders] who read this would prayerfully discern the accuracy of my interpretations and the source of the revelations.

Lord Jesus Christ is my Master. I no longer am. Praise Him.

CASE STUDY 3: THE AUTHOR'S EXPERIENCE

From a government bureaucrat who had been mainly a pew-warmer:

> *When I went to the sanctuary, I was led to pick up the hymnal first — that surprised me, but I followed, and was led to hymns 130 and 131: "God will take care of you" and then "We gather together to ask the Lord's blessing."*
>
> *Clearly, his message was, ask his blessing, discern his will, display faithfulness, and all will be provided. Then he led me to Psalm 40 — more reassurance — what a wonderful experience!*

From a high-school boy:

> *As I stood outside the labyrinth, I saw a journey. An adventure, a decision to follow Christ, and a path to find him. The first few steps were mysterious. How long is the path? Would I ever make it out? I didn't know...*
>
> *As I got a little way down the path, I noticed I was right next to the center, the goal. It was right there, so easy. But a little purple line separated me from it, showed me there were no shortcuts. As I walked on, it seemed like I was getting further from my goal. Though I was closer, I walked along the outside of the maze.*
>
> *I saw others outside the maze staring at me and I was embarrassed. I could have turned around and run outside the maze, but instead I glanced at the center. I saw my prize, though the distance between us seemed to grow, and I pursued it.*
>
> *As I walked on, people would pass by me, separated by that purple line. Some looked like they were ahead of me, or behind me, or going the wrong way. But I couldn't tell, so I had no place to judge them.*
>
> *As I seemed to be going in circles, I eventually reached the center. There, I found God. His gift, His grace, His presence. And now, as*

I glance at the entrance, I know what needs to be done... I can't help others here in my little God circle. I must make another journey, back outside, to share my experience with the world. That way, when the world is destroyed, they can take refuge with me in God's maze and we can worship him all of our days.

And so I leave this place and start a new journey.

(I nailed my plan for my life on the cross, and God gave me his plan for my life. When I traveled through the maze, God showed me life, He showed me how it appears and what to do. Please share this with others, I'm not the only teen who needs guidance.)

From a high-school girl:

I was walking in front of the church, by the corners of [the intersecting roads] and I saw all the people driving by, and many of them probably didn't know or had misconceptions about God. Then I saw the rain headed this way, and this little analogy came to me:

- *All the people were driving home because of the storm, and the rain was already starting in a few drops.*
- *The coming "storm" of God's power will bring many people "home," and it's already beginning.*

Now, I don't know if that was really from God or if that was just me. But I think it would be really good if it were from God. It seemed to fit together a bit too well to be entirely from me, so maybe God's saying this could be if you pray for it. Or it could be — I've never had anything like this happen before and I'm not entirely sure it's not from me because I don't have any experience with this sort of thing.

As far as I know, none of these people had "any experience with this sort of thing." It was clearly a move of God's Holy Spirit.

Revival rejected

But somehow it didn't lead to church-wide revival. Despite the undeniable experiences of God's presence, there was no call to continue the meetings, even on a monthly basis. In fact, within a few weeks the council was back to focusing on the church's financial difficulties. Within four months, discontent among influential members of the congregation had grown to the point that I called a "Town Hall," an open forum for questions and comments, but without decision-making powers. One long-time member who felt she wasn't getting the attention she deserved took the floor to tell me, "You need to stop spending so much time with God and start spending more time with us!"

I wish I could tell you why this happened and how to prevent it in your church, but I can't. Looking back in the years since I have not been able to identify anything I did wrong or should have done differently, although I certainly might have missed something.

My takeaway is that God will not force revival on people who are not willing to accept it, even if at first they think they are. The pastor should not feel guilty if that happens.

Satisfied Christians

In 2007 I was appointed to a "tall-steeple" church in a prominent location in a small city. My first impression was that it was a congregation of old people and their parents. Forty years before, it had been one of the largest and most influential churches in the city, and many of the parishioners were still living in that past. However, as someone said, "No matter how hard you pray, you will never wake up and find that it's 1960 again."

A key aspect of revival is the freedom to move around, whether it's to lay hands on someone in prayer, to dance with joy, or even to be slain in the Spirit. The architecture of the sanctuary mitigated against all of this, with two sections of long immovable pews, steps and an altar rail across the only open space, and solid wooden stalls for the pastor on the pulpit side, the reader on the lectern side, and the choir behind.

For me, though, the biggest obstacle to church-wide revival was the fact that so many members seemed satisfied with where they were spiritually. True, some were dissatisfied with the state of the church, but that was because it was no longer what it had been, not because it was not yet what it could be. Many were wonderful saints with great Bible knowledge and years of following Jesus. Still, there was little hunger for more.

Two examples illustrate this.

About a year after I came, I realized it was the fortieth anniversary of the beginning of the Jesus Movement. I knew that many of the young people who had been part of that had moved away from it as they got jobs, got married, and raised families. Now children were grown and gone, retirement was looming, and many were looking back nostalgically on their youthful idealistic enthusiasm for Christ. It seemed to me a perfect time to try to reignite that revival fire.

I talked about this to the church council, and proposed that we sponsor a Jesus Movement reunion festival featuring bands and speakers from that time. An influential council member was from the next generation older than me. His response was, "You mean you want to invite a bunch of hippies?!" Most of the council had the same negative reaction, and what I believe was a great opportunity was dropped.

The second example is the response of the congregation when

CASE STUDY 3: THE AUTHOR'S EXPERIENCE

genuine revival-like things did happen. On two occasions, several months apart, I invited guest evangelists for evening services. In both cases, the focus of the evangelist was on equipping the saints for ministry (Ephesians 4:12) by teaching them about divine healing and then inviting them to pray for each other. In both services people were healed as other laypeople prayed for them, or as they prayed for other people (James 5:16).

Those healed testified in Sunday church services. Some of the healings made a visible physical difference in the person. The healings lasted. Yet significantly fewer people came to the second meeting than the first. After the second meeting, even with its new healings and testimonies, there was not enough interest to schedule a third.

A similar thing happened with several attempts to hold evening praise and worship services. All I can conclude is that most people were satisfied with their Christianity as it was.

Having said this, there was a small core of people who seemed to catch revival fire. The flame was preserved through a home group called Flowing in the Spirit. I encouraged the ten or fifteen who attended to open themselves to the presence and power of the Holy Spirit, and several of them reported life-changing experiences. However, revival never spread to the entire congregation.

In 2015, after thirty-four years working for revival as a full-time pastor, I felt called to change my ministry focus to writing and took early retirement.

I recount all this to share another side of pastoring revival from the previous case studies. I pray both experiences, the massive outpourings of the Spirit and the trickles of revival, will help equip you.

Dr. Wentz, Student of Revival

One of the first books I read as a pastor, after finishing all the required reading for seminary, was Charles Finney's classic *Lectures on Revival*. I also read Charles H. Spurgeon's *Lectures to My Students*, and historical accounts of Wesley, Whitefield, Cane Ridge, Azusa Street, the American healing revivals, and others. My motivation was not academic but practical. I was a student of revival because I wanted to help my church experience it.

At the height of the River movement, shortly after we began First Corinthians Fellowship, a wonderful older woman in the church offered to pay my tuition and costs toward a Doctor of Ministry degree. I was surprised, not to say shocked, but I gratefully accepted. When time came to select a dissertation topic, I quickly settled on "Pastoring Revival." I had read plenty on revivals in history but very little about what to do when you are in the middle of it.

As mentioned previously, my dissertation adviser recommended a case study of two churches in the River. This involved research, interviews, and visiting the services. Up until this time, my mindset when I visited scenes of revival was to enter in as fully as I could, soak up all I could, and bring it back to my church, both for my own sake and for that of my people. Now I had to step back and try to see things more objectively. I moved from participant to observer. It was a different perspective, but I believe a very valuable one. I would not have been able to compile the recommendations for pastoring revival that make up the rest of this book without it.

Interestingly enough, my D. Min. work was done at Asbury Theological Seminary, the graduate school of the university where the 2023 Asbury outpouring started. When I attended in the 1990s, people still spoke of the revival which struck a chapel service there in 1970. In addition, extended revivals had struck the college in 1905,

1908, 1921, 1950, and 1958. I'm tempted to suggest a study about why one place experienced so many outpourings, but I suspect the answer would be similar to what a Buckingham Palace groundskeeper told a tourist who asked how they got the lawns so nice: "First, begin 400 years ago." Or as Bart Pierce told me, "Where he's been, he'll come again."

I readily acknowledge researcher bias. I believed, and still do, that the River was a wonderful blessing from God, despite the inevitable mistakes which accompany anything in which human beings are involved. However, I do not believe my bias in favor of the River adversely affected my ability to do meaningful research and analysis, or to come up with the conclusions that constitute the remainder of this book.

III

Part 3. Pastoring Revival: Shepherding the Flock Without Getting in God's Way

Be on guard for yourselves and for all the flock, among which the Holy Spirit has made you overseers, to shepherd the church of God which He purchased with His own blood.
— Acts 20:28 NAS

7

Pastoring a Move of God — Isn't That Presumptuous?

I believe the enemy does not want revival to occur in America, and so pastors must guard against his attacks. We must learn to pastor a revival or else run the risk of wandering away from the River. — John Kilpatrick, *When the Heavens Are Brass*

If revival is truly a movement orchestrated by God, isn't it a bit presumptuous for human pastors to inject themselves into it? Why not just sit back and let God do whatever God wants to do?

Wesley Campbell, pastor of New Life Vineyard Fellowship in Kelowna, British Columbia, chose to introduce Spirit-led prophetic ministry to his church in the context of small groups. In *Welcoming a Visitation of the Holy Spirit,* he describes what happened the first time they brought the ministry into the main church service.

The Holy Spirit came powerfully. People responded. Many fell on their faces in repentance. Pastor Campbell writes,

> As this surreal picture unfolded, I was abruptly yanked back to

reality by a man pulling on my pant leg. It was a deacon in our church. He had a look of panic on his face. Desperately he asked, "Wesley, can I go to the bathroom?" I whispered in a hushed tone, "Yeah, sure, go to the bathroom." ... When the supernatural intersects with the natural there exists the possibility for tension. That is why there must always be a leader. Renewal or no renewal, somebody has to be there to say, "It's OK; you can go to the bathroom!"

Most scholars of revival agree that human actions and attitudes, particularly those of the pastor, can kill a move of God before its potential is reached. Being overly controlling and trying to make God's actions fit our theological boxes can quench the Holy Spirit (1 Thessalonians 5:19). Failure to provide Biblical safeguards or trying to use the revival to build our own ministries or reputations can grieve the Holy Spirit (Ephesians 4:30). Either one can bring a revival to an untimely end.

Strike a Balance

There's a balance to be struck between God's initiative and the pastor's oversight. In *The River Is Here,* Melinda Fish writes,

What God is able to do in any local church or city, during this or any season of renewal, depends on the discerning, faithful responses of leaders who have learned above all how to get out of His way and let Him move.

As a pastor, it's humbling to think how many times when God was working I might have been like a four-year-old "Daddy's helper," thinking I was contributing when I was really just in his way.

On the other hand, you can overdo getting out of God's way. John Kilpatrick advises,

> A flock needs a shepherd all the time, so a pastor cannot retreat from his [or her] duties just because God's Spirit has taken over.

Fire is a wonderful thing, if properly tended. If it gets out of the fireplace, it will either die or become destructive.

One Size Doesn't Fit All

Revival won't look the same in every setting. In fact, given the infinite creative diversity of our God, it would be surprising if any two churches experienced revival in exactly the same way. As we've seen, Rock City Church and The Crossing had major differences. Each also differed in many respects from other churches in the River such as Toronto Airport Christian Fellowship and Brownsville Assembly of God — not to mention the churches which experienced revival under the ministries of Jonathan Edwards, Charles Finney, and others throughout history. And all were different from the outbreak that seems to be starting in colleges today.

Clearly, God does not limit his sovereign moves to only one setting. God can bring revival to college campuses, independent Pentecostal churches, traditional mainline denominational congregations, and everything in between. Successful pastors of revival do not try to force their church's experience to mimic any other.

It seems evident that the culture of a given church plays a large part in determining how revival will look in that place. Tommy Tenney certainly believes, from his experience of revival in many settings, that this is the case. There were many aspects of the revival meetings at Rock City Church that were very similar to how they have always "done church" at that place, though they may have become invested with a new sense of spiritual presence. The worship at Washington Crossing changed after the revival began from traditional to contemporary, but it's difficult to know how much of that was a necessary characteristic of revival and how much was just adjusting to the times. Certainly, in almost everything except the manifestations of revival, Washington Crossing remained typical of successful evangelical United Methodist churches across the country at that time.

New People

One of the first effects of revival is an influx of new people. Martin Lloyd-Jones points out in his book, *Revival*, that these new people are not likely to be a homogeneous unit, either with themselves or with the existing members of the church.

> *You get a cross-section of every conceivable type and group in society, irrespective of class, age, temperament and everything else: a most astonishing feature, but one which is found with strange regularity in all the stories.*

And all of these people must be welcomed, often healed, discipled, equipped, and incorporated into the church. In other words, they must be pastored.

Leadership Counts

Other than two years as a missionary in the Georgia colony when he was a young man, John Wesley did not himself pastor a local congregation, but for decades he oversaw Methodist societies that were in revival. In his journal entry for June 5, 1772, he compares revivals in two English towns, Weardale and Everton, on several points. His fifth point of comparison is pastoral leadership.

> *There was a great difference in the instruments, whom God employed in one and in the other work. Not one of those in or near Everton had any experience in the guiding of souls. None of them were more than "babes in Christ," if any of them so much. Whereas in Weardale, not only the three Preachers were, I believe, renewed in love, but most of the Leaders were deeply experienced in the work of God, accustomed to train up souls in his way, and not ignorant of Satan's devices. And hence we may easily account for the grand difference between the former and the latter work; namely, that the one was so shallow, there scarce being any subjects rising above an infant state of grace; the other so deep, many, both men, women, and children, being what St. John terms "young men" in Christ. Yea, many children here have had far deeper experience, and more constant fellowship with God, than the oldest man or woman at Everton which I have seen or heard of. So that, upon the whole, we may affirm, such a work of God as this has not been seen before in the three kingdoms.*

Wesley Duewel's book *Revival Fire* describes a revival in East Africa that began in 1930 and lasted fifty years. In the midst of this move of God,

> some Church of England friends felt someone should be sent to 'control' the revived people, but this could easily have led to grieving and stopping the work of the Holy Spirit. Leadership from within the revival needed to be raised up and guided. Someone from the outside could not as fully understand or as wisely lead.

Revival Fruit

Like any manifestation of true Christianity, revivals will validate themselves by their fruit. Individual Christians will be drawn closer to God and a godly life. Pastors will be encouraged and renewed in faith, hope, and vision. Churches will worship with renewed passion, disciple with renewed understanding, and serve with renewed compassion and grace. Communities will be transformed as Christian values of love and grace are lived out in the lives of those who have been renewed.

Every person, every pastor, every church, and every community need these things. That's why God moves us to pray for revival, it's why he sends it, and that's why it is so important to know how to shepherd your people through it.

8

Acquiring the Fire: Pastoring to Prepare for Revival

Then those who feared the Lord spoke with each other, and the Lord listened to what they said. In his presence, a scroll of remembrance was written to record the names of those who feared him and always thought about the honor of his name.
— Malachi 3:16 NLT

The famous 19th-century preacher Henry Ward Beecher once wrote,

In our church we have had for years an able-bodied committee whose duty it is, when anyone is discovered asleep in the congregation, to go at once into the pulpit and wake up the pastor.

When I asked Bart Pierce why God chose him for the Rock City Church revival, he answered, "God always finds a man that he can 'beat the hell out of.' Then he may be able to use him."

Tommy Tenney added, "God chose Bart because he had been doing the right stuff for a long time, and he was hungry, desperate—not just to do the things of God, but for God Himself. It's getting very difficult to find pastors who are desperate enough for God to abandon all their programs, yet have a heart enough for man that they'll do the programs."

When God chooses where to send revival, it seems he favors pastors who

- fear the Lord
- always think about God's honor and glory
- stay alert
- are humble
- are desperate for God
- have a heart for people

Lightning, Seed, Sharing

Revival is like lightning: you can't make yourself be struck by it, but you can make it more likely that when it strikes, it will strike you. If you want to be hit by lightning, hold a metal pole on a bare mountaintop in a thunderstorm. If you want to be hit by revival, persevere in fervent prayer.

Revival can also be like a seed germinating. In 2015 I retired from full-time pastoral ministry and moved from Maryland to a farm in the Missouri Ozarks. There we began working with the Department of Conservation to transform a former cow pasture into a habitat friendly to birds, bees, and butterflies. We assiduously sprayed to eradicate the imported pasture grasses and seeded with native wildflowers. As the next spring came, we eagerly looked for signs of what we had sown, and we did see some. But we also saw many other plants we had not seeded, all over the field! The conservation agent explained that these were from seeds that lay dormant in the ground waiting, sometimes many years, for the right conditions to sprout. Our preparation had provided the right conditions.

Like a seed, revival may lie dormant for many years. When the right conditions come, seeds scattered years before will sprout, some of them in surprising places.

For example, a friend wrote me of something that happened in his church's prison ministry shortly after the Asbury outpouring. Most of their prison chapel services are apparently rather routine. This time, the leaders felt led to replace the regular live service with a video of one of their home pastor's sermons and altar calls. Oddly enough, it was one that didn't seem to get much response in the church service. But in the prison, as my friend described it, "Thirty or more inmates responded to the showing with confessions and crying and emotional manifestations of God's movement changing their lives."

This was hundreds of miles from Asbury. On the surface it seems completely independent of what happened there. But I believe this and many other incidents are the first fruits of revival seeds that have lain dormant for decades.

Revival can strike like lightning or spring up like a seed, but it can also be carried from one place to another like a carefully tended flame. *So Abraham placed the wood for the burnt offering on Isaac's shoulders, while he himself carried the fire and the knife* (Genesis 22:6 NLT).

Revival flame is carried when people who have experienced it in one place talk or preach about it somewhere else. Pastors who are seeking revival for their church often open their pulpits to such testimonies. But sometimes it's just laypeople talking to their friends about what they've heard and seen in other places. The pastor may know nothing about it until things start happening in a church service or prayer meeting.

The word revival implies a bringing of new life to that which was languishing. New life certainly seems to have been the effect of the move of God in Rock City Church and Washington Crossing. Both were experiencing the aftereffects of major congregational upheavals when revival came.

However, in neither case did revival come at the lowest point. Both churches were on their way back up when the Lord's move appeared. It seems that neither being a dying nor a healthy church is a precondition for revival, but being unwilling to remain in a depressed state may be.

This brings to mind the statements of Pierce and Tenney about being hungry and desperate for God. In Tenney's estimation, maintaining that hunger is the key to maintaining revival. Keeping that hunger alive in the congregation is largely a function of pastoral leadership.

Can you create hunger? Of course you can. The whole restaurant advertising industry is built around that fact. They've done studies. They know the color orange makes people hungry. They know the smell of bacon makes people hungry. They know a sizzling sound makes people hungry. There's even a slogan in the advertising business: "Sell the sizzle, not the steak."

Ask God to show you the spiritual equivalent of orange, bacon, and sizzle for your congregation. You're not manipulating. Jesus said, *Blessed are those who hunger and thirst for righteousness* (Matthew 5:6 ESV). You're just helping them get blessed.

Four Actions

Historically, revival comes in waves. As talk of revival spreads and the spiritual temperature across the country rises, it becomes easier for the dry tinder in other churches to catch revival flame. So how do you raise the lightning rod, stir up the seed bank, or prepare tinder and kindling in your church? Four actions can help you and your people be ready for what God might do.

Pray for revival

If there's one common thread among revivals throughout history, it's a lifestyle and atmosphere of prayer. This could include specifically asking God for revival, but it doesn't have to. Continual prayer opens a spiritual channel between a church and God through which it's easy for revival to flow.

Pastors can't make revival. You can hold special meetings and book famous speakers. If it's your style, you can manipulate emotions and advertise with hyperbolic promises. Those things can generate crowds, but they aren't revival. If we want genuine revival, we have to ask God for it.

When we're praying for revival, all the normal rules apply.

- Pray earnestly: *The earnest prayer of a righteous person has great power and produces wonderful results* (James 5:16 NLT)
- Pray with faith: *You can pray for anything, and if you have faith, you will receive it* (Matthew 21:22 NLT)
- Pray with others: *If two of you agree here on earth concerning anything you ask, my Father in heaven will do it for you* (Matthew 18:19 NLT)
- Pray persistently: *One day Jesus told his disciples a story to show that they should always pray and never give up* (Luke 18:1 NLT)

Preach about revival

Create hunger and expectation in your people by using the power of the pulpit. Revival is not a subject to be covered in one sermon. Here are just a few things you can preach about.

- What revival is and isn't
- The need for revival in our world

- The need for revival in your church
- The need for revival in individual Christians, including yourself (be vulnerable but prayerfully wise here)
- Revivals in the Bible
- Revivals in history
- Current revivals around the world, especially in Africa and South America
- Revivals in the news
- People you know who have experienced revival

If you have experienced revival yourself, by all means preach about it. Just be careful not to let people think you feel like the experience makes you more holy or spiritual than those who have not experienced it, or that others have to experience it the same way you did.

Expose your people to those who have been touched by revival

Most people who have experienced revival love to talk about what God has done. Invite some of those people to speak in your church. They don't have to be famous evangelists or revival leaders, though don't pass if you have an opportunity to host one.

Laypeople can often convey a greater sense of genuine excitement than professional speakers. If it's one of your members, someone your people know, or someone from a neighboring church, that can lend an invaluable sense of authenticity. If they aren't comfortable preaching a whole sermon, or you aren't comfortable turning over the pulpit for a whole service, ask them to give a testimony.

Testimonies are a powerful tool that is underused in most churches. The Bible says, *They have defeated [the dragon] by the blood of the Lamb and by their testimony* (Revelation 12:11 NLT). In particular, testimonies from those who have been involved in revival can have many positive effects.

- They help listeners realize revival is a real thing that happens to real people like them
- They reduce fear of the unknown
- They help people recognize that God can use revival in different ways for different people
- They demonstrate that revival is not just for fanatics
- They can raise the listener's faith: "If revival can happen to that person speaking, maybe it can happen to me!"

Create opportunities for your people to practice acting like revived Christians in a revived church

In 1738 John Wesley returned to England from a failed missionary trip to the American colony of Georgia. Thirty-five years old and an ordained priest in the Church of England, he was so discouraged he began to doubt whether he was even saved. His journal entry for March 6 records this fascinating interchange:

> *I found my brother at Oxford, recovering from his pleurisy; and with him Peter Bohler: by whom (in the hand of the great God) I was on Sunday the 5th clearly convinced of unbelief, of the want of that faith whereby alone we are saved with full Christian salvation.*
>
> *Immediately it struck into my mind, Leave off preaching. How can you preach to others, who have not faith yourself?*
>
> *I asked Bohler, whether he thought I should leave it off, or not? He answered, "By no means."*
>
> *I asked, "But what can I preach?"*

> *He said, "Preach faith till you have it, and then, because you have it, you will preach faith."*

Applying Bohler's advice to revival, it might sound this way: "Act as if you are experiencing revival till you have it, and then, because you have it, you will experience revival."

But wait! Isn't it hypocritical to preach about faith when you don't have it, or to tell your church to act like it's been revived when it hasn't?

Wesley apparently had a similar concern, but he pushed forward anyway.

> *Accordingly, Monday 6, I began preaching this new doctrine, though my soul started back from the work.*

I believe whether it's hypocritical or not depends on your intentions. If you're trying to convince other people you're more spiritual than you really are, that's hypocrisy. But if your goal in acting like a revived Christian or church is to become one, that's not hypocrisy, that's acting in faith. *Whatever you ask for in prayer, believe that you have received it, and it will be yours* (Mark 11:24 NIV).

So what do I mean when I say, act as if you are experiencing revival? I'm not talking about imitating the preaching and activities of whatever big revival may be in the news. Those are just outer manifestations. True revival is on the inside, of a person or a congregation.

When I was young, it was not uncommon for my friends' car batteries to go dead. If they had a stick shift, the solution was a push-start. You put the car in neutral, pushed it until you got it rolling, jumped in, put it in gear, and let out the clutch. If everything went right, the engine fired. Suddenly, instead of you pushing the car, the car was carrying you.

Acting like you're in revival when it hasn't started yet is a spiritual push-start. Lead your congregation to do the things that a healthy, on-fire church does. Whether it be prayer meetings or prison ministry or a new worship style or street preaching or a food pantry or whatever God leads you to do, do it out of faith and obedience as if your hearts had already been changed. I believe you'll experience a spiritual combustion that will take off and carry you and your church *far more abundantly beyond all that we ask or think* (Ephesians 3:20 NAS).

That's what happened to Wesley. Two and a half months after the above experience, he reluctantly attended a Bible study where someone was reading from Martin Luther's commentary on Romans. His journal records,

> *While he was describing the change which God works in the heart through faith in Christ, I felt my heart strangely warmed. I felt I did trust in Christ, Christ alone for salvation; and an assurance was given me that He had taken away my sins, even mine, and saved me from the law of sin and death.*

That was the beginning of the Methodist revival. It and its grandchildren, the Holiness and Pentecostal movements, are still going strong after almost two hundred years.

I'm not saying that if you pray and preach and expose your people to revival and give them opportunities to act like a revived church, God will necessarily send a great church-wide outpouring that draws international attention. That's up to God. Pursue God, not revival, and leave the results to him. *Seek first the kingdom of God and his righteousness, and all these things will be added to you* (Matthew 6:33 ESV).

As I described earlier, in my own ministry First Corinthians Fellowship, the Week of Prayer, and Flowing in the Spirit were all efforts to do what I have described, and none of them resulted in a dramatic community-wide or even church-wide move of God. However, groups within each church did experience revival, and in each case the whole church benefited.

9

Guarding the Flame: Pastoring During Revival

Sustained revival affects a church in various ways. Many members will become personally revived. This may lead them to new ministries, or it may lead them to pursue their old ministries with new zeal and power. Revival may touch the largest part of your congregation, as at Rock City Church and The Crossing, or only a few, as in my own experience.

Some of those not touched will object to some part or parts of the revival, and either try to disrupt it or leave the church.

Still others will appear almost to ignore the revival, continuing their old religious habits in the same way they always have.

It's fun to spend all your time with the revived folks, but you're still the pastor of the whole church, so you have to figure out how to pastor all three groups.

At the same time, new people will come. Depending on what God is doing at your particular church, they may be curiosity seekers attracted by reports of something different or revival-hoppers looking for the next spiritual experience. Or they may be people who know some of your members and see a difference in them, or who were affected by new ministries spawned by the revival.

By and large, the curious and the hoppers won't stay. That's not a failure on your part. They came because they heard about something unusual, and unless God does something new in their hearts, as soon as the next noise happens they'll be off again.

But some didn't just hear about something, they saw something. They saw a changed person in their friend or a changed church in the new ministries. They saw evidence of the ability of God to make not just a noise, but a difference, and they wanted that difference in their own lives. These are the ones who are most open to discipleship.

How do you balance all of this, get God's priorities, lead all the segments of your congregation, continue to deal with the inescapable pastoral fact that Sunday comes every week, and do it all in a way that is sustainable over months and years? In other words, how do you pastor revival?

I don't have any magic answers, but based on everything I've learned as seeker, pastor, and student of revival, here are some thoughts that I pray will be helpful. These are roughly sequential, but there's a lot of overlap. You'll probably have to balance several of them at the same time.

Welcome the Holy Spirit

Do not stifle the Holy Spirit. — 1 Thessalonians 5:19 NLT

Many translations read, *Do not quench the Spirit.* That's a good and accurate translation, but I really like the NLT reading as well. Perhaps it's because I remember watching the TV character Archie Bunker silence his poor wife by yelling, "Edith, stifle yourself!"

It's bad when a man treats his wife that way. It's worse when a pastor treats the Holy Spirit that way. Yet we can do that, all too unknowingly, if we dismiss out of hand anything that doesn't fit our theological box or our ecclesiastical comfort zone.

Don't get me wrong. I'm not saying you should enthusiastically endorse every weird thing that may happen just because somebody claims it's the Holy Spirit. As pastor, you have a duty to guard your people against false claims and misleading directions. But it's also important to maintain a general heart attitude of openness and welcome instead of suspicion or control.

Since ancient times, churches have started their services with prayers inviting God to come and move. Formal liturgies begin with a prayer called an invocation because it invokes the presence of God. Less liturgical churches often just say, "Come, Holy Spirit." The wording is not important. The important thing is a desire to welcome God the Holy Spirit, whose temple the church is, to manifest himself in and among his people in any way he desires.

I love the story in Acts 12 when the angel breaks Peter out of prison. Peter goes to Mary's house, where he knows the church has been praying for him, and knocks on the door. When Rhoda answers, she's so shocked to see him, she slams the door in his face! The prayer leaders aren't much better; they tell her she must have seen a ghost! So much for *Whatever you ask for in prayer, believe that you have received it, and it will be yours* (Mark 11:24 NIV).

My point is, if you've been inviting the Holy Spirit to come to your service and one day he shows up, don't slam the door in his face. Invite him in and make him welcome.

Even in revival, your church is made up of human beings. That means there will inevitably be some things you will have to guide, correct, maybe even rebuke (2 Timothy 4:2) if you want the Holy Spirit to feel welcome. If you are truly seeking to follow his guidance as you do this, the result will be even greater freedom, love, peace, joy, and all the Spirit's fruits.

Work to inculcate this attitude not only in yourself but in your congregation as well. I can tell you from sad experience that the Holy Spirit can be quenched and grieved by the people in the pews as easily as by the person in the pulpit.

Explain What's Happening

> *These people are not drunk, as some of you are assuming. Nine o'clock in the morning is much too early for that. No, what you see was predicted long ago by the prophet Joel.*
> — Acts 2:15–16 NLT

Imagine you are walking down the street in Jerusalem on Pentecost morning. Suddenly you hear a noise that sounds like a hurricane, but there's no wind. Then you see flames coming from the upstairs windows of a house, but there's no fire. Then a bunch of fishermen and women from Galilee rush down the stairs and start shouting in strange languages. Wouldn't you want somebody to explain what in the world is going on?

What God sends to you is not likely to be as dramatic as the Jerusalem Pentecost. It's not even likely to be as dramatic as what happened at Asbury. Perhaps people will start crying, or laughing, or testifying, or prophesying, or speaking in tongues, or rushing to the front for prayer. Whatever it is, it will be different from what your members are used to, and those not caught up in it will want to know what is going on.

In Acts 2, Peter explained. Let's look at what he did and said as a model for how you might explain revival when it happens in your church.

- *He was filled with the Holy Spirit* (verse 4). Don't try to explain things in your own power or intellect. Ask God to put the words in your

mouth. After all, they're his actions you're explaining.
- *He stepped forward* (14). Peter was probably as awestruck and overcome as everyone else, but he was a leader. There's a reason the lists of Jesus' followers usually start with his name (see Acts 1:13 and 15). Peter saw the confusion, he heard the negative rumors starting ("They're drunk!"), and he took action. As pastor, when your congregation is confused and rumors start flying, don't let it mushroom. You're the leader. Step forward.
- *He stood with the other leaders* (14). Yes, you're the pastor and you're the one who has to speak up, but if you have other leaders with you it will make things a whole lot easier down the road. That may not be possible if revival breaks out suddenly (though if you've given them this book to read it will certainly help). But as time goes on and things in your church start to change, having your leaders share your vision and stand with you can be a lifesaver.
- *He got their attention* (14). Peter had to shout to get everyone's attention. You just need to not let go of the microphone. Don't interrupt what God is doing, but if others try to interrupt or hijack it, speak up, calm things down, and return control to the Holy Spirit.
- *He spoke with calm authority* (14). In modern pastoral parlance, he was a non-anxious presence. His stance, his stature, the tone of his voice, all conveyed reassurance. People thought, "Hey, there's somebody who seems to know what's going on. He doesn't seem worried. Maybe it's not the end of the world after all." What's happening may be as new to you as it is to everyone else, but at least you've read about similar things. In the words said over me at my ordination, "Take thou authority!"
- *He squelched the negative rumors* (15). After getting the crowd's attention, Peter's first concern was to stop the gossip. It's fallen human nature to assign a negative meaning to things we can't

understand. Before saying what was happening, he clarified what was not. He didn't just make a counter-statement: "No, they're not drunk." He added a reason to believe: "It's too early for that. It's only nine in the morning." If unusual things start happening in your service people probably won't think everyone stopped by the local bar on the way to church. They're more likely to think people have suddenly become fanatical, or been hypnotized, or contracted mass psychosis. Whatever they think, you need to reassure them that nothing bad is going on.

- *He cited Scripture* (16). Whenever you explain something spiritual, you're on solid ground if you can cite a Scripture for it (in context, of course). Notice that the passage Peter quoted didn't address the particular phenomena of the morning — the rushing sound, the tongues of fire, the unknown languages — but Peter was still able to make the connection. This side of Pentecost, our task is easier, because we have the New Testament as well as the Old.
- *He turned the focus to Jesus* (22-36). Peter didn't try to explain everything that happened in detail. Instead of focusing on phenomena, he turned the focus to Jesus. The Holy Spirit doesn't talk about himself or his activities, he testifies of Jesus (John 15:26). As you explain what's happening, don't try to satisfy people's intellectual curiosity. You won't be able to fully, and that's not the real point anyway. Your goal should be to inspire a spiritual hunger for a deeper experience of God.

The need to explain things doesn't stop with the initial events of revival. Whenever something unusual happens you should be ready to explain it, as best you can, both to those who are there and those who will hear about it later.

For instance, any time you sense a special atmosphere in the room, others will as well. But if you don't tell them what it is and that you sense it, too, they may think it's just something in their head. The lessons from Peter's address in Acts 2 apply here also. It can be very helpful to say something like, "God is here. I can feel his presence." Or, "Do you sense something in the air, a special kind of atmosphere? That's God." And go on to build their faith: "When God makes his presence known like that, expect something to happen." Or, "God is making himself available to us in a special way. If you have something on your heart, this might be a good time to talk to him about it."

Remember, you don't have to satisfy everyone's intellectual curiosity, especially when it comes to speculating about why God might or might not be doing something. Just being able to give something a label and cite precedence — from the Bible, reports of other revivals, or your own experience — is all the explanation most people need.

And if revival causes you to make changes to business as usual, whether it's adding services or changing music or introducing testimonies or anything else, it's helpful to add Peter's method to your normal process of introducing change.

Your First Set of Decisions

In the Introduction, we looked at the first set of decisions Kevin Brown, President of Asbury University, had to make when revival broke out in a chapel service. When revival comes to your church, you will also be called on to make some decisions.

If it happens suddenly in a church service, as it did with Rock City Church and The Crossing, many of your decisions will be similar to those faced by Dr. Brown. If you're working to import revival, as I did throughout my ministry, there will be a different set of decisions.

If God takes you by surprise

You're leading your congregation through a normal worship service, and suddenly it's not a normal service anymore. Perhaps someone interrupts verbally, or starts acting in a strange way. Perhaps testimonies are a normal part of your service, but today they are unusually long, or powerful, or plentiful. Perhaps half the church responds to the altar call.

Your first responsibility as pastor is to discern whether what's happening is a human-initiated distraction, however well-intentioned, or whether it's God breaking into your service. The difficulty is that even when it is God, he still works through humans saying and doing things.

This is a good time to silently pray one of my favorite prayers: "Help!" Then shepherd your flock, trusting that God will not let you lead them astray as you decide:

- Will you call things to order and go on with your normal pattern of worship, make adjustments, or abandon your worship plan altogether?
- If someone wants to speak, will you give them the platform, will you ask them to tell you what they want to say and then decide, or will you just deny the request, at least for this service? If you let them speak, will you give them the microphone or keep holding it yourself?
- If you are recording or live-streaming the service, will you continue, curtail recording, or keep recording but cease live-streaming until later review?
- If things still seem to be happening as your normal dismissal time approaches, will you extend the service? I have found it effective to say something like, "It's X o'clock, so if you have to go you may, but

God seems to be doing something unusual here so if you can stay longer I encourage you to do that." Also remember other people or activities that could be affected by an extended service, such as child care workers or another activity that needs the worship space.
- Will you schedule a special service, perhaps that evening, for those who want to pursue what happened? If not, how will you follow up? How will you publicize it, and to whom?

If you're importing the flame

A sudden outpouring of the Holy Spirit is exciting, and God can do it anywhere at any time. However, that experience is limited to the relatively small number of people who happen to be in a given church service when it happens, or who can travel to that location for follow-up services. For everyone else, the revival flame is carefully carried from another place, stoked, and tended. If you are one carrying revival from a place you've been, or hoping to light a match, your decisions will be different.

- How will you prepare your people? Will your preaching and public prayers focus on revival? If so, in what way?
- Will you try to bring revival into a regular worship service, or schedule special services?
- Will you speak yourself, invite testimonies from laypeople, or invite a guest preacher?
- What will be the marks of revival you teach and look for? Is there anything you will particularly encourage or discourage?

Set Some Ground Rules

Ground rules are basic policies that keep you from having to make decisions about the same questions over and over. They can save a lot of time and avoid a lot of trouble. You can't foresee every possible issue, but it's a good idea to think ahead of time about possible situations and how you will want to deal with them.

You probably have some ground rules in place already, even if you don't call them that. They are the practices that are so ingrained in your congregation that members think of them as "just the way you do things." And they make sure new folks learn them! Things like the unwritten church dress code, whether you allow food or coffee in the sanctuary, what kind of outside groups or activities are allowed to use your building, what kinds of decorations are allowed in the worship space, and so on. Unless your congregation is a brand new church plant, these are things that have grown up gradually over time as now and then a new question arose.

Revival brings a lot of new questions all at once. Hence the need to consciously create a new set of ground rules.

So what kind of ground rules do you need? Here are just a few of the areas you might want to think about.

- Who is authorized to speak on behalf of the church?
- Will you limit service length?
- Will you set a curfew time for evening services?
- What will be your attitude toward visitors from other local churches?
- What rules might you want about people taking photos or videos, including sharing or streaming on social media?
- What rules might you want about using names or other personal information on social media?

In thirty-eight years of ministry, I never ceased to be amazed at what some people seemed to consider appropriate things to say in church or post online. I suggest you consider ground rules that prohibit:

- Political speech
- Arguments about theological or eschatological opinions
- Implying that people who don't come to revival services are less spiritual than those who do
- Implying that revival means your church is better or more spiritual than others
- Implying that certain revival experiences are necessary for salvation or to be a good Christian
- Urging people to leave their church and come to yours

As pastor, you might want to consider some personal ground rules as well. One issue faced at Asbury was outside "revival experts" who offered to take over what was happening. Most of these were, no doubt, sincerely well-intentioned people who felt that their experience could be helpful. If revival at your church garners some publicity, you could be on the receiving end of similar offers, not only from revivalists, but from denominational officials as well. If you have an appropriate measure of humility, it can be tempting to defer to their presumably greater expertise. However, God sent this revival to your church, not theirs. And he sent it to revive your church, not their ministry. Think and pray carefully about how God might want you to respond if such an offer comes your way.

Be Open to New Experiences

An important principle of revival leadership is openness to whatever new things God may want to do. John Kilpatrick wrote,

> *As God takes us "from glory to glory," He will also take us out of our comfort zones. When new and different things happen, we must be careful that we rejoice, and enter into all God has for us. If not, we may never taste of the next "glory" God is bringing.*

"New and different" is a mild description of some of the things that happened in River services. Kilpatrick himself was at first uncomfortable with many of the manifestations which occurred in his church. After he began to experience some of them personally, he became "more hesitant to stop and hinder others from doing the same."

As we've mentioned, people who experienced the previous revival may bring those responses and manifestations to the next one. This is not necessarily good or bad. My attitude is to be open to anything that is not clearly unbiblical unless God guides me otherwise.

So what does "unbiblical" mean? Some would say that anything not specifically authorized or exemplified in the Bible is unbiblical. Carried to its logical conclusion, that would rule out live-streaming, pipe organs, and even church buildings. But the Bible says, *Wherever the Spirit of the Lord is, there is freedom* (2 Corinthians 3:17 NLT). One of God's major attributes is creativity. God will never go against his word, but he loves to do new things. So I don't consider anything unbiblical unless it directly violates a biblical command or principle.

Again, we come back to 1 Thessalonians 5:21–22: *Examine everything carefully; hold fast to that which is good; abstain from every form of evil* (NAS).

Welcome New People

I saw a cartoon depicting the chair of the pastoral search committee summing up the meeting: "So we're agreed. We want a pastor with dynamic, creative, forward-thinking new ideas that will attract more people just like us."

Unfortunately, that kind of thinking doesn't just exist in cartoons. Most normal methods of outreach depend largely on encouraging our members to invite their friends and neighbors; in other words, more people just like them. However, when revival breaks out, things are different. We've already quoted Martin Lloyd-Jones' observation in a previous chapter, but it bears repeating:

> *You get a cross-section of every conceivable type and group in society, irrespective of class, age, temperament and everything else: a most astonishing feature, but one which is found with strange regularity in all the stories.*

A lot of these folks won't look or talk like your members. Some will almost certainly violate some of your unwritten rules. Heaven forbid, one might even sit in the church matriarch's seat! Most of your members won't intentionally try to make visitors feel unwelcome, but it's equally true that most won't realize how unwelcoming they can seem without trying.

I don't need to tell you how to welcome visitors, or how to encourage your people to be welcoming. I'm just pointing out that in a revival situation it can be more important than usual to devote some time to intentional teaching on the subject.

Reassure the Fearful

After one Sunday morning service, a woman came up to me all aflutter. "Pastor!," she said, "You've changed everything!"

I wasn't aware of any big change. I asked what she meant.

"The offering used to be before the sermon, but today it was after!"

One of the most natural and prevalent human emotions is fear of the unknown. Almost as prevalent among religious people is fear of having their spiritual security shaken. Revival can prompt both of these fears.

I was probably twenty years into being a pastor before I figured out why so many people are so resistant to even small changes in the worship service. It's because, for many, the Sunday morning routine is their main or only connection to God. If the routine is changed, their connection to God is threatened. That's scary.

At the same time, revival often involves events or feelings people have not experienced before. This can be frightening for those to whom it happens directly. It can be even worse for those who only hear reports of the crazy things that are happening in "those new services." Has their pastor gone crazy? Is the church turning into a bunch of religious fanatics?

Usually, these fears can be allayed simply by addressing them, gently but directly. A soothing explanation, bolstered by testimonies from trusted church leaders, is probably all that is necessary.

Keep an ear open for specific concerns people may have. For every person who talks to you about something, probably many more silently feel the same way. For that reason, it's a good idea to make your reassurances publicly rather than just in private conversation with those who come to you.

Educate the Skeptics

The modern western worldview teaches us to doubt anything that can't be measured, replicated, and explained scientifically. Unfortunately, this attitude is often deeply ingrained even among faithful churchgoers. We are all subliminally conditioned to be skeptical of things of the spirit.

The answer to skepticism is education. When people understand that something is a known phenomenon and they're given reasons to believe, skepticism often disappears.

In many ways, education is just an extended explanation. As such, you can follow the outline of Peter's Pentecost explanation in Acts 2. Depending on your preaching style, you could do a topical series on revivals in the Bible and history, an expository series on revival passages in the Bible, or a narrative series on your and other people's personal experiences with revival.

I do recommend that you use your sermons for this education rather than a Bible study or adult Sunday School class, just because the questions probably run more widely than the attendance in those groups.

For those who remain unconvinced after your best efforts to educate them, perhaps they belong in the next section.

Silence the Cynics

There will be those who refuse to believe anything good about what is happening in your church despite your best efforts to explain, reassure, and educate. Fear is natural and skepticism can be healthy, but cynicism is nothing but destructive.

If you've been a pastor for more than a few months you've probably encountered your share of gripers, whiners, and complainers. Cynics, critics, accusers, and nay-sayers can ruin your church's morale, not to mention your own. Revival, especially at the beginning, can be a flickering spark. It needs to be carefully tended, not covered with a wet blanket.

Paul wrote to Titus,

> *There are many rebellious people who engage in useless talk and deceive others. . . . They must be silenced . . . So reprimand them sternly to make them strong in the faith. . . .You have the authority to correct them when necessary, so don't let anyone disregard what you say.* (Titus 1:10-13; 2:15 NLT)

You have biblical permission, even an obligation, to restrict these people's platform for spreading negativity. If possible, get your governing board or appropriate committee to stand with you; that may take some educating of your leaders.

If the troublemakers threaten to leave, ask them to close the door on the way out. You can't allow anyone to hold God's work hostage to their threats.

I realize those are strong words. I guess it's because I've seen how much damage people can do when they want to control the church instead of welcoming what God is doing, or at least trying to understand it.

Communicate With Other Pastors

It's an odd thing, but if it's not approached right, revival in your church can be threatening to the pastors of other local churches. This is especially true if you haven't developed a good, trusting relationship with them beforehand. It's easy for some pastors to see excitement and increased activity in your church and fear that their own members will be drawn away.

It can be tempting to see other churches as your competition, but I don't have to tell you that's not the case. Your competition is the mattress, the fishing hole or golf course, children's sports, and everything else people could be doing on Sunday morning. The fact is, nearby pastors can and should be your greatest support and resource.

Other than your spouse, only another pastor can understand the joys and stresses of ministry. Only another pastor can give you advice that is actually relevant to ministry. The only person who really knows how to pray for a pastor is another pastor. And when it's not wise to open up to a member of your congregation or someone in your denominational leadership, another pastor can be there for you.

Certainly laypeople can pray for you. Certainly laypeople can share insights and encouragement. Certainly God can speak to you through laypeople. But being responsible to God for the spiritual well-being of a group of his children is a unique challenge. You need close relationships with others who share that burden.

Note: I'm not talking about the local ministerium that meets monthly to drink coffee and decide who will host the next community Thanksgiving Eve service. Those are fine as far as they go, but usually they don't go nearly far enough. I'm talking about pastors who will be open and honest with each other and really pray together.

If you haven't developed this kind of relationship with at least a few other pastors in your area, don't wait for revival or a natural disaster or some other kind of precipitating event. Do it now.

You and the other pastors in your area should already be doing these things:

- Praying together
- Coordinating church activities so you don't all schedule Vacation Bible School the same week
- Planning joint community activities or mission events to demon-

strate the unity of the faith and take advantage of strength in numbers
- Warning each other about con artists going the rounds
- Telling each other if someone from their church suddenly starts attending yours, especially if they are bad-mouthing the church or pastor they came from

This creates a basis of trust for when revival comes to your church. Then you can:

- Share what's happening, so they aren't going on rumors
- Talk about how to handle their members who visit your revival
- Discuss theological perspectives
- Learn from any who may have revival experience
- Offer any help you can in spreading the revival to their church

Prioritize Among New and Existing Ministries and Resources

As time goes on and the revival continues, you will have to plan and prioritize accordingly. If the revival draws visitors they may bring new resources, but that is not always the case. Your musicians, your ushers, perhaps your childcare workers, whoever cleans the bathrooms and takes out the trash, and you yourself, have limited amounts of energy. In the initial excitement everyone may run on adrenaline, but that can't continue indefinitely. In the beginning you may postpone or cancel committee meetings and other activities in favor of special revival services, but eventually you will need to reschedule them.

Don't assume that because God is inspiring the revival, that means everything else should be sacrificed to it. Presumably, God also inspired the good ministries you were engaged in before. Revival should enhance these, not replace them. The new move may provide impetus to cancel some hold-over relics that no longer represent effective ministry, but that kind of evaluation should take place periodically whether or not revival is happening.

This is not the place to get into how to go about planning and prioritizing ministries. (My book, *Pastoring: The Nuts and Bolts*, goes into detail about that among other things.) I just want to remind you that if you're not careful, revival can quickly deplete your limited resources. Before that happens, it's important to work through your normal church decision-making processes to agree on priorities and make some contingency plans.

Be Willing to Make Changes

Revival changes people's hearts. That heart change may need to be reflected in other kinds of changes.

One example is the change in worship style at Washington Crossing. At the time revival broke out, the church's worship featured traditional hymns and organ music. Once the revival was established, the hymnals and organ were replaced with praise music and a contemporary band. That's about as big a change as a church can make, but the pastor and congregation were willing to make it.

Martin Luther was willing to question traditional practices. Charles Finney was willing to embrace then-unorthodox "measures" to promote revival. Willingness to change and the ability to lead a congregation through change are important elements of pastoral leadership at any time, but especially in revival.

Members who are not involved in the revival may tell themselves this is only a phase you are passing through, and things will soon return to normal. Proposing changes to worship services or other church operations implies that you intend this weird new stuff to be permanent.

That can inspire some strong opposition. As with any other changes you propose, it's important to seek God's wisdom in the timing, in getting appropriate backing from leaders and influencers, and in how you communicate the reasons for the change and its benefits.

Keep Ministering to the Late-Adopters

Revival is by definition a new thing for the congregation. Like any new thing, acceptance and adoption can be roughly plotted on a bell curve. A few will be enthusiastic right from the start. As time goes on, more and more will adopt the idea. Some will hold out a little longer, and a few may never get on board.

Remember that those who don't get involved are still part of your flock, and you are still their pastor. They still need and deserve your attention, and their opinions and desires still count. Whether or not they ever become supporters of the new thing, as long as they are not actively opposing what God is doing, you need to support them.

Guard Your Character

Ron McIntosh devotes several chapters of his book, *The Quest for Revival*, to the personal qualities of revival leaders that help sustain or cut short revival. He sums up his findings by writing that the key is "the character that makes up the private area of our lives. That is what causes the momentary flow of God's Spirit to become perpetual."

He says the greatest enemy of godly character is success.

> [People] will pray and fast, seek God, and wait on His favor in trying moments, but once the breakthrough comes, they strangely become self-sufficient. Somehow, they begin to believe the adulation of men and become "doers" for God instead of "receivers"

from God.

In *Overcome by the Spirit*, Francis MacNutt describes how this can happen, and offers some advice from his own experience. He is writing specifically about the slain-in-the-Spirit phenomenon, but his words are good to remember regarding all the manifestations of revival:

> *If you find that people fall over when you pray for them, egotism and vanity are certainly temptations you will have to conquer. . . 'Slaying people in the Spirit' is certainly a temptation to pride — one of the most spectacular manifestations the ministry can offer. It is dramatic, it is connected with me, it is visible. I need to work to counteract in my own spirit any desire to show off. I have to develop a sense of detachment about whether or not it happens at a given meeting — and certainly resist any effort on my part to make it happen. Nor must I allow myself to feel inadequate when it doesn't happen (the flip side of pride). . . . Those of us who pray need to remind ourselves, too, that people's resting in our services is not a sign of holiness on our part.*

Here are a few reminders as you guard your character:

- Pursue holiness
- Be humble
- Be transparent
- Be accountable
- Be appropriately vulnerable
- Listen to constructive criticism and pray about it
- Ignore anonymous and destructive criticism; despair can destroy your character as easily as pride
- Don't steal sheep

- Don't steal God's glory
- Be overly careful and accountable about money and sex
- Specifically authorize one or two people to call you out whenever they sense something you should address

I encourage you to ask a few trusted people in your congregation to create a pastor's prayer group, praying especially for your character, wisdom, and energy. *Preyed On or Prayed For* by Terry Teykl and *The Prayer Shield* by Peter Wagner are helpful books about how to do this.

Protect Your Key People

Sometimes we pastors don't realize the sacrifices of time and energy our key people make. Adding revival services to your normal schedule puts demands on your musicians, your ushers, your audio-video people, your custodian, your childcare workers, whoever counts and deposits offerings, and others. Usually they are happy to do it at first, especially if they are experiencing revival in their own lives. However, as time goes on and it begins to look like extra services are transitioning from something special to the normal routine, it can become wearing. Many of these people have a spiritual gift of helping (1 Corinthians 12:28), which means they are unlikely to complain or even let you know they are being overworked. It's your responsibility to be aware and guard them from burnout.

Here are some ways to protect your key leaders and workers:

- Publicly recognize and thank them
- Make a habit of asking them how they're doing
- Set up a schedule that will spread the load
- Stick to the schedule so they can count on time for other things
- Make sure they prioritize their families

- Disabuse them of the notion that doing God's work somehow means they don't need to take care of their physical, mental, and relational health
- Teach them the importance of rest
- If you don't already have one, create a systematic process for identifying, recruiting, training, equipping, deploying, and supporting new people in these roles

Guard Your Flock

One of the main responsibilities of a shepherd is to guard the sheep. Revival can mean less danger from things like spiritual apathy, but it can increase other risks — and often the new dangers are ones that most pastors are not used to having to look out for. For example:

- Guard against pride: "God sent us revival! That must mean he loves us more than the other churches!"
- Guard against complacency: "God sent us revival! That means we've arrived! We don't need to work on being spiritual anymore, we've already reached the top!"
- Guard against division: "We go to the revival meetings a lot more than they do. That means we're more spiritual than they are. That means our ideas are more Spirit-led than theirs are. That means it's our spiritual duty to squash their ideas by any means possible!"
- Guard against thrill-seeking: "People at that church have cooler miracles than in our church. I'm going to start going over there!"
- Guard against presumption: "God's blessing us with revival. That must mean if we go way out on a limb and build a new building, God will pay for it!"
- Guard against wolves in sheep's clothing: "This new person says they have more experience in revival than our pastor, and they

pointed out some concerns about our pastor that I never noticed before. I'm going to start going to this new person's Bible study so I can learn the stuff our pastor isn't telling us."

Keep Feeding Your Spirit

Acts 2:4 tells us that on the day of Pentecost 120 disciples were filled with the Holy Spirit. Acts 4:31 tells us they were filled with the Spirit again. Acts 4:8 says Peter was filled with the Holy Spirit in between those times.

In Ephesians 5:18, Paul instructs Christians to be filled with the Holy Spirit. He uses the Greek present tense, which means a repeated or continual action rather than a one-time experience. It could appropriately be translated as "be being filled" or "continually be filled."

Why do we need to continually be filled and refilled with the Holy Spirit? I heard a great answer to this question once, and I wish I could remember who said it. The answer is: "Because we leak."

That's not a bad thing. Leaking the Holy Spirit all over is what Christians are supposed to do. Jesus said, *"Whoever believes in me, as Scripture has said, rivers of living water will flow from within them."* John explains, *By this he meant the Spirit, whom those who believed in him were later to receive* (John 7:38–39 NIV).

But you can't keep pouring out if nothing is pouring in. You need to keep your spirit fed.

It's hard enough for pastors to feed their spirits under normal circumstances. You can't go sit under another preacher because you work on Sundays. You can't read the books you want to because you're too busy reading the books you have to. Even your Bible reading can too easily become sermon research instead of spiritual sustenance. And with meetings and counseling and hospital visits and administration and worship planning and you name it, who has time to sit and soak in God's presence for an hour or two? Add the responsibilities of pastoring a revival on top of that, and it's no wonder your spirit could dry up.

You can't let that happen. Your number one responsibility to your congregation is to stay in touch with God.

We commonly refer to pastors as shepherds, but the fact is we are under-shepherds. Jesus is the shepherd. We pastor the flock on his behalf. If we are not spiritually in a place where we can reliably be led by his Holy Spirit, we are derelict in our duties. You have to feed your spirit.

Just as a refresher, here are a few ideas about how to do that:

- Go on a retreat
- Journal
- Engage a spiritual director
- Watch or listen to recorded services
- Attend revival meetings at other churches
- Pray with other pastors regularly
- Declare a moratorium on electronics for a day or two
- Read faith-building books
- Try a Christian spiritual practice from outside your tradition
- Read or write poetry
- Listen to or sing psalms, hymns, and spiritual songs (Ephesians 5:19)

Remember the Sabbath

We may not all agree on what day the Sabbath is, or what we should or should not do on the Sabbath, or even whether keeping a Sabbath applies to us in the New Covenant. However, I hope we can all agree that God told his people to follow his example of taking one day out of seven to rest, and that he did not think it out of place to put that instruction in the same list that addresses issues as serious as stealing, adultery, and murder.

In other words, taking a break now and then is not a sin. It might even be one of the Ten Commandments.

Can I be honest with you, pastor? I have to tell you something you may not want to hear: if you take a day off, your church won't fall apart. Your people won't drift away. Revival won't stop. They can get along without you for a little bit.

But if you don't take time to rest, you might fall apart. Your passion might drift away. Your physical heart might even stop. You can't get along without rest.

For some reason, taking time off seems to be one of the hardest things for pastors to do. And when revival comes, it seems even harder. But that can be when it's most important.

I remind you again: Charles Finney, who knew a little something about revivals, said one of the main killers of revival is physical exhaustion of the leaders.

'Nuff said. Go take a nap.

From Revival to Revived

If revival is an intervention by which God breathes new life into a church, like spiritual cardio-pulmonary resuscitation, then it should be a temporary phenomenon. When the church starts breathing on its own, CPR is no longer needed. This is the view Bart Pierce espoused when I interviewed him twenty-four years after the outpouring at Rock City Church.

If revival is a state of openness to the Holy Spirit, enthusiasm for worship, and a focus on living out the gospel, it should be the normal state of the church. This is what Scott McDermott meant when he told me The Crossing is still in revival after two decades.

The difference is obviously a matter of definition. The question I want to look at here is this: if there is something you are doing during revival, such as holding additional services, that is not a sustainable part of your normal church activities, how do you know when to stop? And when you do stop, how do you keep your church from sinking back to its pre-revival state?

The simple answer to the first question is, God will tell you when to stop any special revival activities. He may speak directly to your heart, as he did with Bart Pierce; he may speak through circumstances, as when key participants in First Corinthians Fellowship moved away; he may speak through your church governing board in your normal decision-making process; or he may speak in some other way. One of the main results of revival should be to make you and your people more open and receptive to the leading of the Holy Spirit. Trust his leadership in this decision.

The second question has a simple answer as well. You keep your church from sinking back to its pre-revival state by being a good pastor. Preach the gospel. Pray. Love the people. Model holiness. Administer wisely. Keep growing your spirit. These are all things you should already know. Just faithfully do them, and God will take care of the rest.

10

Don't Water the Spark: Avoiding Revival Killers

The story is told of a prayer meeting in a little country church. A deacon stood up and prayed fervently, "Oh Lord, send us a spark of revival. Just a little spark is all we need, Lord. Send us a spark!" A farmer chimed in, "Yes, Lord, and water that spark!"

I'm sure God knew the farmer wasn't asking for revival to be doused, but unfortunately, that can be the result of some well-intentioned pastoral actions.

Revivals can be and often are cut short, ending well before they have accomplished God's full intention for them. That's not always the pastor's fault, but sometimes it can be.

- *You can kill revival by quenching it,* dampening people's faith and enthusiasm through over-caution and over-analysis
- *You can kill revival by starving it*, failing to provide the teaching and support it needs
- *You can kill revival by claiming it,* trying to use it for your own glory
- *You can kill revival by over-controlling it,* usurping God's role in deciding what should happen when and how

When I first started talking about this book, several people advised me not to write it because previous revivals had been "pastored to death." Trying too much to control everything can quench or grieve the Holy Spirit.

On the other hand, Rick Joyner writes in his study of the Welsh revival of 1904-5 that in their determination not to allow that to happen,

> *Evan Roberts and his colleagues allowed the enemy to push them too far, so that they actually prohibited the organization that was needed to help preserve the great advances that were made. Because of this, just a couple of years after the revival, evidence of it was scarce, and the whole nation quickly drifted back to its former depravity.*

Pat Kaveny, a veteran revival pastor and international conference speaker, says the problem is not that revivals are pastored, but that they are pastored by the wrong people. Some believe their experience with previous moves of God qualifies them to direct the next one. Often those in the next move humbly accept those claims and abdicate their leadership. The result can be a poor imitation of what God did last time instead of the power of what God is doing now.

Baptist pastor Paul Wellinghoff adds another reason revivals may end too soon.

> *Many discussions and books have been written about why particular revivals died, stopped, or gradually dissipated over time. I believe the answer, in a nutshell, is that those revivals became about the revival and not about discipleship. Many revivals have, in turn, led schools of revival when we need schools of discipleship instead. The Apostles didn't spread the fire of Pentecost; they*

> *spread the gospel and made disciples. Love the move of the Spirit and remember the Spirit was given to us to help make disciples.*

When revival breaks out in your church, you can be tempted to concentrate so much on the needs of the revival that you fail to meet the ongoing needs of your congregation. This can cause your members to rebel against the revival to the point of snuffing it out.

Conversely, you can spend so much effort on the existing members of the congregation, perhaps especially those who oppose the revival for one reason or another, that the revival dies of neglect.

No one with a true pastor's heart can be content to sit and enjoy revival within the church while ignoring the needs of those all around. An inward focus on the needs of the congregation to the exclusion of those outside is a sure way to short-circuit any move of God. John Wimber, founder of the Vineyard churches, wrote,

> *God [is] pouring out his blessing. But if we don't dig the channels, if we don't go out into the highways and by-ways, if we don't put evangelism forward, if we don't do the things God calls us to do, then revival won't spread.*

Rick Joyner uses the analogy of pioneers versus settlers.

> *The spiritual pioneers usually do not like or understand the spiritual settlers, but both are needed for lasting spiritual advancement. . . . If the settlers do not allow the exploration of new places, the corruption of stagnation will settle in. If the explorers do not tolerate the settlers, no one will ever benefit from all of the new places they find.*

The River revival lasted longest in churches where pastors struck a proper scriptural and Spirit-led balance in these areas. Some did it by relying on guest preachers to conduct revival services, leaving the pastor free to focus on the needs of the congregation. Other leaders moved from emphasizing physical manifestations, which could be off-putting to some church members, to accepting them without focusing on them, instead stressing an intimate love relationship with God—"seeking his face and not his hand." Pastors and revival leaders all over the world used the then-new internet communications technology to share accounts of what God was doing so that, if something unusual happened, the pastor could know if it had happened elsewhere and move forward with more discernment.

John Arnott, John Kilpatrick, and Melinda Fish, all leaders in the River revival, have written from experience about the things that can make it hard to keep revival alive. Taken together, their lists include apathy, disappointment, discouragement, distractions, doubt, fear, public denunciation, and pride.

These hindrances to revival can arise from within a congregation, even one experiencing a move of God, at least as often as they come from outside. John Kilpatrick observes,

> *Satan not only blinds the minds of unbelievers, but he especially tries to distort and destroy God's work in the heart of sincere followers (2 Corinthians 4:4; John 8:44).*

In his classic book, *Revivals of Religion*, Charles Finney listed twenty-four "Things Which May Stop a Revival." Almost two hundred years later, only number eighteen no longer applies. (I have my own opinion as to what should replace it, but without data relating it to revival, I won't name it here.) I've included just Finney's headings; he adds at least one paragraph of explanation to each.

1. A revival will stop whenever the Church believes it is going to cease.

2. A revival will cease when Christians consent that it should cease.

3. A revival will cease whenever Christians become mechanical in their attempts to promote it.

4. The revival will cease, whenever Christians get the idea that the work will go on without their aid.

5. The work will cease when the Church prefers to attend to selfish concerns rather than God's business.

6. When Christians get proud of their "great revival," it will cease.

7. The revival will stop when the Church gets exhausted by labour.

8. A revival will cease when the Church begins to speculate about abstract doctrines, which have nothing to do with practice.

9. When Christians begin to proselytize.

10. When Christians refuse to render to the Lord according to the benefits received.

11. When the Church, in any way, grieves the Holy Spirit.

a. When Christians do not feel their dependence on the Spirit.

b. The Spirit may be grieved by a spirit of boasting of the revival.

c. So, too, the Spirit is grieved by saying or publishing things that are calculated to undervalue the work of God.

12. A revival may be expected to cease, when Christians lose the spirit of brotherly love.

13. A revival will decline and cease, unless Christians are frequently re-converted.

14. A revival cannot continue when Christians will not practice self-denial.

15. A revival will be stopped by controversies about new

measures.

16. Revivals can be put down by the continued opposition of the Old School, combined with a bad spirit in the New School.

17. Any diversion of the public mind will hinder a revival.

18. Resistance to the Temperance reformation will put a stop to revivals in a Church.

19. Revivals are hindered when ministers and Churches take wrong ground in regard to any question involving human rights.

20. Another thing that hinders revivals is, neglecting the claims of Missions.

21. When a Church rejects the calls of God upon it for educating young [people] for the ministry, it will hinder and destroy a revival.

22. Slandering revivals will often put them down.

23. Ecclesiastical difficulties are calculated to grieve away the Spirit, and destroy revivals.

24. Another thing by which revivals may be hindered is censoriousness, on either side, and especially in those who have been engaged in carrying forward a revival.

Many of these problems manifest themselves in the lack of good leadership. In his journal entry for June 12, 1774, John Wesley analyzed the demise of revival in Weardale after only two years. He wrote:

1. Not one of the Preachers that succeeded was capable of being a nursing-father to the new-born children:

2. Jane Salkeld, one great instrument of the work, marrying, was debarred from meeting the young ones; and there being none left who so naturally cared for them, they fell heaps upon heaps:

3. Most of the liveliest in the society were the single men and women; and several of these in a little time contracted an inordinate affection for each other; whereby they so grieved the

Holy Spirit of God, that he in great measure departed from them:

4. Men arose among ourselves, who undervalued the work of God, and called the great work of sanctification a delusion. By this they grieved some, and angered others; so that both the one and the other were much weakened.

Hence, the love of many waxing cold, the Preachers were discouraged; and jealousies, heart-burnings, evil-surmisings, were multiplied more and more.

The pressures of ongoing revival can expose cracks and weaknesses in character which can bring down a pastor and choke the movement. Ron McIntosh traces the pattern in the life of 19th-century evangelist John Alexander Dowie, who started well but fell into financial improprieties:

Success gave way to pride, pride led to self-sufficiency, and that made him "too big" for consultation with his peers. Lack of a fraternal fellowship left him too open to criticism, and his reaction to criticism in the later years was bitterness. . . . He also no longer simply proclaimed the Gospel, but spent an inordinate amount of time defending himself.

McIntosh lists other traits of fallen ministries, including pride and glory-seeking, which lead to manipulation and exaggeration of results, and "diversion of funds to purposes other than those for which they had been solicited". He expands on the latter:

Money tied up in things not ordained by God is a scheme of the enemy to destroy ministries. Money poured into ministry is for influence, not affluence.

Finally, McIntosh states, "The number one killer of revival is lack of rest." This was point seven in the list above from Charles Finney, who went on to comment,

> Revival will stop when the Church gets exhausted through its labor. Multitudes of Christians make a mistake here in times of revival. They are so thoughtless and have so little judgment that they break up all their habits of living, neglect to eat and sleep at proper hours, and let the excitement run away with them, so that they overdo their bodies, and are so imprudent that they soon become exhausted, and it is impossible for them to continue in the work. Revivals often cease from negligence and imprudence, in this respect, on the part of those engaged in carrying them on, and declensions follow.

McIntosh sums up: "Overwork leads to exhaustion, exhaustion leads to impropriety, and impropriety leads to a fall."

Bart Pierce intentionally alerted himself and his staff to all these dangers. He distributed Finney's list to his staff and led them in a study of it, so they could work together to avoid these obstacles. His division of labor with Tommy Tenney allowed him to concentrate on church matters without getting exhausted by also preaching the revival meetings.

Scott McDermott did not take such explicit steps to avoid revival killers, but his leadership style emphasized the kind of attitudes and actions that keep revival going. In particular, he periodically took members of his staff and key laypeople to visit the revival at the Toronto Airport Christian Fellowship, where apathy, doubt, and other destructive forces were replaced by renewed enthusiasm.

An outpouring that does not spread to nearby churches can be a birth pang of a revival whose full time has not yet come, but it can also be the fault of neighboring pastors who water the spark and put out the fire. Ignoring what God is doing, or responding with doubt, fear, envy, or criticism, will certainly keep revival from spreading to their church. If these attitudes become pervasive in the community they can even seep in to quench revival in the church where it started.

11

Putting It All Together

What follows is based on thirty-eight years of pastoral experience as well as the case studies and literature reviewed in this book. Of course, most of these conclusions are not absolutes. Ask God to give you the proper balance for what he is doing in your situation.

Leadership

Does pastoring revival require different skills than pastoring a church not in revival? Does it require different skills than pastoring a church to bring it to revival? Given the short duration of local church revivals in the past, the answer to both these questions is probably yes. Seeking revival may require special skills in preaching and teaching. Sustaining revival calls for additional skills in pastoral care and administration. Fortunately, these are all things that can be learned, and every pastor should continually be learning them.

While Bart Pierce and Scott McDermott are different in many ways, they share certain characteristics with other successful pastors of revived churches. Many of these are the same characteristics which contribute to pastoral success in general: good leadership qualities, prayerfulness, and a desire to seek and follow God's will. These are particularly important given the difficulty of pastoring different groups in a church which respond to revival in different ways.

Two pastoral traits stand out as crucial to keeping a revival going. The first seems obvious: a view of revival as a desirable, even normative, state for the church. The second necessary trait is the willingness and ability to take actions specifically designed to maintain revival. Here are some ways these traits reveal themselves in practice.

- Recognize that while a revival is a sovereign move of God, the people and church experiencing it still need to be pastored.

- Be confident of your vision as a leader. Put in whatever time it takes in prayer and study to justify that confidence, then continually cast and recast the vision to keep it before your people.

- Lead by example in prayer, gentleness, encouragement, vulnerability, and openness to God.

- Recognize that pastoring a church in revival can be more difficult than pastoring at other times. Make this a subject of study, and seek help with pastoral and leadership skills as needed.

- Lovingly and non-judgmentally continue to pastor those who are not receptive to the revival.

- Be sure to keep preaching and teaching the whole counsel of God, with Christ at the center and fruitful Christian lives as the goal.

- Watch for or create opportunities for the revival to be expressed beyond the church walls, especially in acts of mercy and justice for the poor.

- Work closely with your music team and any pastoral staff, keeping the vision of revival before them.

- Be prepared to pay the price for revival. This may include disruption of normal routines, changes in perhaps long-standing traditions, increased workload for you and others, and misunderstanding and opposition from within and without the church.

- Prayerfully consider staffing and administrative changes that may be needed to meet the new and continuing needs of the church.

- Don't allow the revival to become institutionalized. Resist the temptation to think of it as a means to build up your own reputation or your church's finances or statistics.

- Be open to whatever God wants to do. Don't restrict God's work by seeking some particular form of revival.

- Study and teach the things that can hinder revival, and take steps to avoid them.

Revival Meetings

A subtle form of "putting God in a box" is seeking to make God's move in one place conform to the shape of God's move somewhere else. This is one of the great temptations of pastoring, especially when one church is receiving public acclaim for its success.

Certainly, there are general principles for effectively pastoring revival, and pastors should seek to learn and apply them. In fact, that is the motivation behind this book. But it is probably safe to say that one of the soundest of those principles is never to try to copy in entirety and detail what another pastor is doing.

Applying principles is important; borrowing certain specific methods may be effective; but seeking to replicate an entire move of God removes the focus from God to what he has created in some other place.

PUTTING IT ALL TOGETHER

- If the revival began as one extended 24-hour-a-day meeting, recognize that such a schedule is not sustainable without careful planning and that God may not want it to continue that way. Prayerfully consider whether and how to transition to a schedule that will meet the physical needs and secular obligations of those involved, and the ongoing other needs of your church and its members.

- Prayerfully consider whether revival meetings should normally be preached by you as pastor, by someone else, or by a team that may include you.

- When someone other than you as pastor preaches the revival meetings, be sure there is mutual understanding as to the respective roles and boundaries.

- Do not expect any revival to be exactly like any other revival, even in areas such as the amount of emphasis on intercession, repentance, or worship.

- Recognize cultural differences in how revival is manifested, and avoid unnecessary affronts to your congregation's sensitivities.

- Neither discourage nor unduly emphasize physical manifestations. Recognize that they often accompany revival but do not produce or validate it.

- When physical manifestations or prophetic utterances occur, exercise scripturally informed prayerful discernment.

- Prayerfully strike a balance between unquestioningly accepting everything that is claimed to be of God and accepting only what fits your preconceived notions or prior experience.

Personal Considerations

- Avoid the temptation to start doing for God rather than receiving from God.

- Jealously guard your personal spiritual life from increased time demands. Don't assume that merely being present in the revival meetings will meet all your spiritual needs.

- Be aware of the legitimate needs of your body, mind, and emotions for rest and recreation outside the revival context. Teach the same to your family and your church workers, and give them opportunities to meet those needs.

- Be aware if your hunger for revival begins to wane. Renew it through prayer, retreat, and reading about or visiting other revivals.

- Be aware that revival often brings increased opportunities for improprieties or accusations of them. Take steps to safeguard against such things, especially those involving money or sex.

Beyond the Local Church

- Publicly support what God is doing in other churches and movements. If you have reservations about another ministry, privately express them to the leader in a spirit of love (Matthew 18:15-17).

- Determine that you will deal with critics of the revival with forgiveness and prayer. Don't allow them to distract too much of your time and attention.

A Personal Request

Thank you for reading this book. If you have friends who might be interested in it, please mention it to them or post about it. The best way to help others find it is to leave an honest review. Just a sentence or two is all it takes.

Thank you!

Final Thoughts

While God uses and indeed inspires many different specific revival practices in many different places, the principles that bring sustained spiritual health and growth are precious few and very basic. In fact, they may all be boiled down into one, a life principle first stated almost two thousand years ago: *Seek first the kingdom of God and his righteousness, and all these things will be added to you* (Matthew 6:33 ESV).

Prayer, openness, and obedience, all in pursuit of God's will no matter where it may lead: these are the keys to successfully pastoring revival.

Appendix: Foundational Principles

Many authors who have written about revival included a list of principles they believed are foundational. Here are some of those lists.

John Arnott

Taken from *The Father's Blessing*.

- Stay hungry for more of God
- Count the cost then pay the price
- Step out in God's strength
- Ask God for answers then run with them
- Go for the kingdom!

Arnott adds,

> If we want God to continue moving as He has, and if we want to allow Him to take us further, we must love to see God do things His way and not attempt to steady the ark (1 Chronicles 13:9).

Steve Beard

Taken from *Thunderstruck: John Wesley and the Toronto Blessing*.

- We should be supportive of movements of the Spirit, even if they are different from what we are accustomed to experiencing.
- We should check out what is happening outside our circles.
- We should become flexible enough to allow God to work however he may choose in a given situation.
- We should be careful to not grieve the Holy Spirit by incorrectly or prematurely attributing what may be a move of God to either human nature or the devil.
- We should diligently test every spirit.
- We should spread the good news of what God is doing in the lives of men and women.
- We should be gentle with those who may be tempted to extremism, especially with the spiritually immature who are touched in the midst of powerful moves of God.

Wesley Campbell

Taken from *Welcoming a Visitation of the Holy Spirit*.

- Spreading the renewal of loving God
- Unity in the faith
- The spiritual disciplines of prayer and intercession
- Prophecy
- Praying for the sick

Roger Helland

Taken from *Let the River Flow*.

- Teach and preach on the biblical, historical, and current experiences regarding renewal and revival.
- Help people to experience and learn firsthand and to overcome fear and wrong perceptions.
- Work with your key leaders and those being touched in key ways.
- Seek after and emphasize the fruit.
- Establish boundaries and protocols for meetings and ministry times.
- Continue to preach and practice the whole counsel of God with Christ at the center.
- Pastor the flock of God in and beyond renewal.
- Continue to provide outlets for ministry and encourage an outward versus an inward focus.
- Be prepared for resistance, criticism, opposition, and "the cost."
- Train your prayer people and prophetic people.
- Do not model or promote an anti-intellectual spirit.
- Above all, lead by example. Be proactive and preventive. Pastor the church as elders and shepherds of God's flock.

John Kilpatrick

Taken from *When the Heavens Are Brass*.

- Persistent prayer
- Building a proper foundation
- Expecting God to move
- Yielding to His Spirit

- Learning to pastor the outpouring
- Continuing to pray for the harvest

About the Author

Best known internationally as author of *Pastoring: The Nuts and Bolts*, in print in seven languages, David Wentz has a passion for helping people connect with God and make a difference. Combining 38 years as a pastor with a first career in engineering and graduate degrees from three very different seminaries (charismatic, mainstream, and Wesleyan-evangelical), he expresses God's truth in ways everyone can appreciate.

Raised in the Episcopal church, Dr. Wentz has also been part of Nazarene, Pentecostal Holiness, and non-denominational congregations. As a Methodist pastor he served small, large, and multicultural churches in rural, small-town, suburban, and urban settings, served as a regional church consultant in the Maryland – D.C. area, and led workshops for pastors internationally. In 2015 he retired to the rural Ozarks, where he writes, works in God's great outdoors, and oversees Doing Christianity, Inc., a small non-profit devoted to equipping pastors in developing and minority-Christian countries.

In 1974, David married his college sweetheart, Paula. They have five children and fourteen grandchildren.

The book of Ezekiel describes David's calling. Twenty-five hundred years ago God called Ezekiel to teach God's ways and proclaim the Holy Spirit, the one who revives dry bones and forms them into a dwelling for God and a source of living water that heals nations.

Bones are still dry today. God still wants to dwell among his people. Nations still need healing. And people still need to be taught God's ways and be moved by God's Spirit. David calls that "Doing Christianity," and it motivates everything he writes.

You can connect with me on:
- https://www.pastordavidwentz.com
- https://www.facebook.com/profile.php?id=100064901162331

Subscribe to my newsletter:
- https://mailchi.mp/e1fdccea2750/doing-christianity-newsletter-signup

Also by David Wentz

My passion is equipping pastors and helping people connect with God to make a difference.

Pastoring: The Nuts and Bolts

The book that trains thousands of pastors around the world. It's not just for rookies!

Comprehensive, cross-denominational, cross-cultural, giving options and best practices instead of dogmatic assertions, and solidly grounded in Scripture, *Pastoring* starts with God's purpose for the church and gives advice from experience on the pastor's personal and family life before thoroughly addressing more common topics like worship, preaching, leadership, and administration. Dr. Wentz also addresses issues unique to charismatic and Pentecostal churches not usually covered in this kind of book.

In seven languages and counting, thousands of print copies have been provided free of charge to pastors in developing and minority-Christian countries, along with an unknown number of digital shares. Every purchase helps support this free distribution.

Pastoring: The Nuts and Bolts Application Guide

A companion to *Pastoring: The Nuts and Bolts,* this small book uses insightful questions to guide you in turning what you learn in *Pastoring* into a comprehensive, personalized, custom action plan for your personal life as a pastor and your professional life leading the church. Not just a one-and-done resource, these questions should be revisited every five or ten years, or at any significant change in your ministry or your church, to give you not only new vision, but a process to get there.

When Church Stops Working: Meeting With God in Your Living Room

One of the most effective ways for pastors to increase their outreach and influence is to train their people to establish a network of house churches. This book, originally written for laypeople who have left the institutional church, has proven to be an effective step-by-step guide for creating such networks.

John Wesley's "The Character of a Methodist"

John Wesley in modern language — ideal for small groups!

Pentecostal, Holiness, Salvation Army, Methodist, and Wesleyan churches all trace back to John Wesley. In a time of upheaval in the Methodist movement, this classic explanation and defense by its founder is required reading. The 18th-century language is updated, references to no-longer-relevant theological disputes are deleted, and an introduction sets the work in context. The result is a clear, easy-to-read text that is enjoyable and understandable for modern readers of all levels of theological interest and expertise. Includes:

Discussion questions
How to lead small groups
Suggested six-week schedule
Scriptural allusions footnoted
Wesley's original version included

www.ingramcontent.com/pod-product-compliance
Lightning Source LLC
Chambersburg PA
CBHW030550080526
44585CB00012B/329